WHAT YOUR ASSOCIATION NEEDS TO KNOW
ABOUT X, Y, AND Z

THE
NEW
RECRUIT

SARAH L. SLADEK

Andover,
Minnesota

ISBN 13: 978-1-931945-66-0
ISBN 10: 1-931945-66-7

Library of Congress Catalog Number: 2006939160

Printed in the United States of America

First Printing: December 2006

10 09 08 07 06   5 4 3 2 1

Andover,
Minnesota

Expert Publishing, Inc.
14314 Thrush Street NW,
Andover, MN 55304-3330
1-877-755-4966
www.expertpublishinginc.com

To my husband, Bradley.
You are my inspiration in all that I do.
Thank you for believing in me.

Contents

Acknowledgements

Thank you to the numerous association executives who were willing to be interviewed or submit information for the purposes of this book.

Thank you to my editor, Sharron Stockhausen, whose insight and guidance helped me to write a better book.

I would also like to thank Barb Ernster for her countless hours conducting research and interviews, as well as Dawn Freadhoff for her research assistance. Writing this book would have taken me twice as long to complete without their dedication and help.

Preface

In 2002, I was working for the Minneapolis Regional Chamber of Commerce as the director of communications and media relations. I attended a national conference for association executives in Florida, and at the general session in a room of four hundred people, the speaker asked everyone under the age of forty to stand up. I was one of about a dozen people who stood up.

I was twenty-nine years old at the time.

The speaker went on to talk about the future of membership associations and the fact that so few young professionals were being invited to lead. The people sitting at my table—all over the age of forty—exchanged knowing glances and cracked a few jokes about their associations' aging board of directors. No one seemed to take the concept very seriously.

And why would they? There are enough Baby Boomers to lead membership associations for at least another decade, maybe even two.

And who would want Gen Xers anyway? That generation has been branded as the slackers. They have no work ethic or ambition or goals. They can't be relied upon to lead.

And Gen Y? Well, they're just kids. They can't contribute anything to the well-being of a professional association.

Right?

Wrong.

Since the beginning of time, young people have had to earn their worth. Young people didn't gain the credibility or respect of their elders until they reached a certain age, had put their time in, and earned their right to speak up, make decisions, and get the attention of others.

But then something changed. Younger generations started learning faster and working harder. The vast majority are now well-educated, world travelers with considerable work experience—all before the ripe old age of twenty-five.

All of a sudden, younger generations have outsmarted their elders and have something meaningful to contribute.

All of a sudden, membership associations need younger members to survive.

While researching this book, it was fascinating to learn how my generation—Generation X—and the generations that follow are changing history. It's also fascinating to learn that so few associations realize that change is even taking place.

When it comes to the way membership associations serve their members, the differences between what the Boomers want and what the Xers want is vastly different. So different, in fact, membership associations will never be the same again.

The passage of the Boomers will mark the end of a chapter in association history. (The first chapter, really, since membership associations have operated much the same way since the sixteen hundreds.)

And yet, few associations are making efforts to recruit younger generations, much less to understand what these generations want and why they are so vastly different from other generations.

That's why I call this book *The New Recruit*. Everything about the younger generations is new and different, from their values and expectations to the way they communicate and spend their time. What worked in the past for membership associations won't work for the younger generations. These are New Recruits because a whole new approach is required.

This book is based on five years of research, experience, and observation. Numerous association executives and consultants were interviewed and several shared their ideas and success stories. Special thanks to all of those people who took the time to share their expertise, insight, and experiences for the purpose of writing this book.

The only succession plan a membership association is the continuation of its membership. I wrote this book with the intention of helping membership associations realize the value that younger members bring, and to ensure their future success.

Yes, the Baby Boomer generation has sustained membership associations for quite some time. But that era is nearing an end, and it's time to start thinking about the next generation of association executives, board members, and volunteers.

Change is never easy, but it is inevitable if you want to succeed.

THE NEW RECRUIT

"This revolution needs a new generation."
—Sarah L. Sladek

Thomas Jefferson once said, "Every generation needs a new revolution."

As substantial numbers of Baby Boomers begin to exit the workforce, membership associations are realizing the need for their own revolution.

Most membership associations remain almost entirely governed and supported by the Baby Boomer generation, and few have or are developing plans and strategies to cushion themselves from this massive exodus of board members, committee chairs, and dedicated volunteers.

In a 2005 electronic survey distributed to eight hundred membership associations nationwide, a whopping 94 percent of the respondents indicated that less than 50 percent of their active membership is under the age of forty.

For more than two centuries, the inner workings and overall purposes of membership associations remained the same. Technology dramatically changed the existence of membership associations in the 1990s, but that hurdle pales in comparison to the generational shift that's about to take place in the twenty-first century.

The passage of the Baby Boomers will mark the end of an era, the end of the membership association as we know it. As this book is being written in 2006, most membership associations believe they have approximately twenty years to coast until all the Baby Boomers have retired.

But that's being overly optimistic. Membership associations that refuse to implement change and interest younger members have a ten-year life span—at most.

I equate the generational shift taking place within membership associations to the invention of electricity. As soon as electricity was invented, everyone wanted it. There was a new and better way of using light, just as there is a new and better way to build your membership—and it starts with recruiting younger members.

Those associations that fail to engage the younger generations will age noticeably and eventually become obsolete. If you don't believe me, visit an association whose membership is largely *under* the age of fifty, and then visit an association whose membership is largely *over* the age of fifty. You will see the difference for yourself. It's the difference of a home with electricity and a home without it. One association exudes energy, while the other association struggles to see what lies within and before it.

The Boomer generation, as the generations before it, is fiercely loyal to membership associations. Boomers tend to view membership associations as opportunities to build beneficial relationships, effect change, make a difference, and help others. They want a successful career, and they want to make the world a better place, and membership associations are one place where they can do both.

Younger generations, on the other hand, refer to membership associations as outdated and irrelevant. Why? Because membership associations don't provide anything meaningful or relevant to them.

In an effort to reinvent themselves, membership associations are scrambling to offer new and improved member benefits, investing in new technology, and trying desperately to remain the premier catalysts for their fields.

And while all of these initiatives are justifiable and important, when it comes to recruiting younger members, most of these tactics are quite ineffective.

The associations that are taking this band-aid approach are the associations I refer to as being Boomer-centric.

The Boomer-centric associations still think they can launch something new and it will resolve all their recruiting woes. These associations have overlooked the simple fact that the vast majority of their membership will retire in the next decade or two—and the generations to follow are radically different from the generations of the past two centuries.

Membership associations have not experienced anything like this before. Generations X and Y have completely different values, interests, needs, and wants from the generations before them. Their worldview, their priorities—everything about them is different as a result of their social experiences.

Generations X and Y will not respond to the recruiting efforts of the past. An entirely new approach is required.

There's no such thing as a quick-fix solution here. A membership association can't just go out and launch a blog and expect the younger generations to come running. Everything about the membership association has to change. Everything requires a new and different approach, which you will learn more about in the following chapters.

There are two types of associations evolving now. The Boomer-centric associations will refuse to change or they fear change. These are the associations that are considered endangered species and likely will be extinct by the year 2020.

The New Recruit associations realize the need to recruit and retain younger members and invite younger generations in to help them make the change. These are the associations that will succeed and survive.

Which association do you want to be?

Borrowing from Jefferson's quote, perhaps it is more accurate, when referring to membership associations, to say: "This revolution needs a new generation."

QUIZ

Before reading the next chapter, take this quick quiz to find out how much you know about the generations. The answers are on the next page.

1. **Which group is the largest?**
   A. Baby boomers (born 1946-1964)
   B. Generation X (1965-1976)
   C. Generation Y (1977-1997)

2. **Between 2000 and 2010, which age group will grow the fastest?**
   A. 25-54
   B. 55-64

3. **True or false?**
   Seventy-five percent of Generation Y have working mothers.

4. **True or false?**
   Generation Y rejects hype and brands the way Generation X did.

5. **True or false?**
   Generation X and Y both see the Baby Boomers as their competitors in the workplace.

Answers

1. If you guessed Baby Boomers, you are wrong. Baby Boomers make up roughly 78 million Americans, which is a huge population bulge, but dulls in comparison with Generation Y, which tops 80 million (25 percent are immigrants). Generation X only accounts for 48 million people.

2. If you said the 55 to 64 group was growing faster than the younger set, you were right. According to the U.S. Census Bureau, growth of the 25-54 population will be only 1.2 percent, while the 55-64 population will be at 47 percent. In other words, the workplace is getting older, faster than we can replace them with experienced workers.

3. True. And 25 percent also come from single-parent homes. Generation Y is an independent group that expects flexible, family-friendly work environments.

4. False. This group is picky and brand sensitive. They expect customization to their individual needs. After all, this generation is used to buying customized jeans on the Internet and burning their own CDs.

5. False. Generation X and Y see the aging work force and smell opportunity. An interesting side note: Gen X trusts Gen Y the least out of all the generations. Gen Y trusts their grandparents and is also closer to their Baby Boomer parents than Gen X is to their parents.

UNDERSTANDING X, Y, & Z

TWO

"I don't think it's fair to say that someone who is thirty-five years old in 2006 thinks the same way as someone who was thirty-five in 1976. Generations have observed profound changes in the world during the last twenty years and make sense of the world differently."

—Jeff De Cagna, membership association consultant

Simply stated, if your organization is actively recruiting individuals over the age of forty, then it's time for a New Recruit.

I refer to Generations X and Y as New Recruits because they will not respond to the recruiting efforts of the past. An entirely new approach is required.

So the first step to successfully recruiting younger association members is gaining an understanding of why their values, interests, needs, and wants differ so much from the generations before them.

The New Recruits, ages eleven to forty-one as of 2006, are marrying, having children, and buying houses on the upper end, and attending junior high on the lower end. They represent a diverse segment of the population, with minorities accounting for a large share of the whole. Few New Recruits have experienced the death of a parent, a mid-life crisis, or a major illness. They are driving the high-tech world and becoming an increasingly positive force in the economy, earning and spending much more than the generations before them.

Understanding this demographic is the most important and toughest challenge today's membership organizations face. It is important because Generations X and Y are the succession plan for today's associations. The challenge exists because Generations X and Y and their older counterparts have very little in common.

"Most membership associations are comprised of mid to older Baby Boomers, and the generations they're trying to attract—Xers and Millennials—have a much different value composition. The organizations are facing a communications challenge to reach younger people because they're operating in a whole different context," stated Susanne Bowman, co-owner of a membership consulting firm.

Jeff De Cagna, a membership association consultant, added that one of the biggest dangers to the vitality of membership associations is their broad generalization of and assumptions about the younger generations.

"I hear it all the time about these generational issues. Generation X doesn't join. We don't know enough about Generation Y, and somehow the Baby Boomers are a sainted class," he said.

What it all boils down to is the Boomer-centric association views the generational differences as a significant barrier to growth, while the New Recruit association views the differences as an opportunity to grow.

The Generations Defined

Where do the generational differences derive?

Largely from social experiences. Think about how much the world has changed since 1946, when the youngest Boomers were born, to 1995, when the youngest Yers were born. These generations encompass nearly a fifty-year time span, and the experiences of each generation vary considerably.

The following are worldview descriptions of persons born within the following age ranges, although the exact dates of birth defining each age demographic are highly debated.

Traditionalists *Born 1926-1945*

The stock market crash, Great Depression, World War II, and Korean War greatly influenced this generation, which grew up in the era of hard manual labor and job short-ages. They would rather do without than borrow money to pay for anything, and they rarely question authority.

Loyal to a fault, Traditionalists–also known as The Silent Generation–expected to build a lifetime career with one employer, or at least in a single field, and make a lasting contribution. Management held all the power and was usually comprised of Caucasian males.

They've always been good and loyal supporters of associations. They can be tremendous mentors to younger generations.

Baby Boomers *Born 1946-1964*

The end of war brought better economic times for families. Baby Boomers experienced their formative years during one of the most wondrous times in America, when the country experienced lots of hope and opportunity. More high school graduates started attending college and the jobs reflected this trend by offering more positions to college graduates only.

On one hand, the Boomers are very much a "Me" generation; they are driven by the desire to achieve great success. Defining themselves by their work and careers, Boomers are the workaholic generation. The goal of the Boomers included a stellar career, and they worked diligently to achieve the corner office, title of president or CEO, and the respect of others. They could dream big and achieve their dreams by simple, honest, hard work.

That's the foundation for the Boomers' attitudes toward their careers and their lives.

On the other hand, Boomers are also very much a "We" generation; they believe in teamwork, in something bigger than themselves. They embrace the Peace Corps mentality of wanting to help others, and they have always felt empowered, engaged, and socially active, largely due to the people and events that shaped their lives: President John F. Kennedy, Dr. Martin Luther King Jr., civil rights, women's liberation, the moon landing, and the Vietnam War.

Boomers tend to view membership associations as opportunities to build relationships, affect change, make a difference, and help others.

Generation X *Born 1965-1981*

When it comes to Generation X, membership associations seem perplexed by this unique and dramatically different generation, which is not joining organizations in the numbers or with the same enthusiasm and commitment as prior generations.

Though popularly associated with the people born during 1961-1981, in the broader socio-economic perspective, the concept of Generation X describes those people who grew up in a period of transition, beginning with the end of the Vietnam War to the fall of the Berlin Wall and the end of the Cold War. Thus, the experience of a global transition between colonialism and globaliza-

tion brings together roughly two diverse generations—
the Baby Boomers and the Baby Busters, also known as
Generation X.

Generation X is just the opposite of Boomers in
nearly every way—and understandably so. The following social experiences heavily influenced the mindset of
Generation X:

- **Gen X grew up with overworked, absen-tee parents.** Xers had the most difficult childhood passage in American history. In the 1970s the feminist movement began to open legitimate career doors to the moth-ers of Gen X kids for the first time. They became the nation's first latchkey kids as more mothers entered the workforce. Their parents were the first to attempt to balance parenthood and dual careers, so many Xer kids saw their workaholic parents suffer from fatigue, illness, and divorce. In fact, Generation X experienced the highest ever divorce rate amongst their parents. The divorce rate and the percentage of children born outside of marriage in the United States doubled between 1965 and 1977. In the 1970s, 40 percent of all marriages were ending in divorce.

- **Gen X grew up with few positive role models.** The 1970s introduced thirty years of massive layoffs in America, and many

Xer kids saw their parents laid off despite their good, faithful, loyal work. At the same time, the nation's leaders, like President Richard Nixon and Reverend Jim Baker, were lying and failing to deliver on their promises. Those instances, coupled with their divorcing parents, led Generation X to become distrusting of hierarchy and authority.

- **Gen Xers grew up feeling isolated.** Prior to Generation X, the generations shared the media. The Baby Boomers watched *The Ed Sullivan Show* and other family-friendly shows with their parents. In 1980, cable television arrived, and most Xers passed their formative years with their own TV channels, like MTV. Many households could afford two television sets, so this was the first generation of kids to spend time watching TV in a second room with a second TV set. This was a totally different media experience and it completely isolated Gen Xers during their formative years.

What do these social differences mean to membership associations? It's the outcomes of these social differences that make Generation X very different from their Baby Boomer predecessors.

For example, membership associations often write off Gen Xers as being slackers and criticize them for not being active volunteers or participants. But because they were children of overworked, absentee parents, Gen Xers place a high value on their personal and family time. They are very selective about how they spend their time and who they spend it with.

Likewise, being raised with so few positive role models, Gen Xers have to feel a sense of trust and belonging before joining any organization. They aren't just going to jump on the bandwagon—membership associations will have to spend more time and effort building relationships with them and gaining their trust.

Growing up in front of a television, and eventually a computer, also had an effect on Gen X. While Baby Boomers like socializing and networking, Gen X would prefer meeting in small groups or having discussions via e-mail. Membership associations continue to focus on offering monthly programs and events, which provide the sense of sorority and fraternity Boomers welcome and embrace, but won't necessarily appeal to Gen Xers.

The membership associations that do not take the needs or interests of Xers into mind will have a very difficult—if not impossible—time recruiting them. And what makes perfect sense to the Baby Boomers simply doesn't apply to Generation X.

Chuck Underwood, a generational consultant, describes the difference between Generation X and the Baby Boomers this way:

"When you think of the Gen X mindset, think of the TV sitcom *Friends*. *Friends* had these serious and recurring episodes in which one cast member would talk in pain and hurt about their formative years with Mom and Dad, and it wasn't played for laughs. Most of their parents hurt them badly. The result of that hurt is what brought them all together. The theme of the show is perfect for Gen X: 'The job's a joke, you're broke, but I'll be there for you.'"

Generation Y *Born 1982-1995*

Membership associations are just beginning to discover Generation X, much less Generation Y. In fact, most organizations make the mistake of assuming everyone under the age of forty falls into the Generation X category—but Generation Y carries its own unique characteristics and a stronghold on America's social landscape.

Whether you call them "Generation Y," "Echo Boomers," or "Millennials," they make up nearly a third of the U.S. population, and spend $170 billion a year of their own and their parents' money.

There are nearly 80 million Gen Yers. This is the largest generation of young people since the 1960s, and they're called "Echo Boomers" because many are the genetic offspring and demographic echo of their parents, the Baby Boomers. Generation Y is already one of the must studied generations in history by sociologists, demographers, and marketing consultants. Why? Because Generation Y is a reflection of the sweeping changes in American life over the past twenty years.

They are the first to grow up with computers at home and in a five-hundred channel TV universe. They are multi-taskers with cell phones, music downloads, and Instant Messaging on the Internet. They are totally plugged-in citizens of a worldwide community, spending more time on-line than watching television. They are connected, but not on an interpersonal level as much as a virtual one.

Generation Y is the most sophisticated generation ever when it comes to media. They create their own Web sites, make their own CDs and DVDs, and are cynical of packaged messages. They rely heavily on word of mouth or buzz marketing from friends and trusted sources—including celebrities. They watch their own television network, the CW, and shop their own stores with multimedia presentations and disc jockeys to lure them in the door. It's a generation used to being catered to. In fact, Generation Y is also the most protected, supervised, provided for generation in history. From when they were toddlers, they have been belted into car seats and driven off to some form of organized group activity. They have been shuttled to playdates and soccer practice with barely a day off by parents who've felt their kids needed structure and a sense of mission.

Most have never ridden a bike without a helmet, ridden in a car without a seat belt, or eaten in a cafeteria that serves peanut butter. They have always been rewarded for participation, not achievement. As a result, this is a generation that has aimed to please and receive the positive feedback of others—parents, friends, teachers, and college admissions officers. Due to the structure in their young lives, they are likely to struggle with taking initiative, thinking long-range, or delaying gratification. They come with a sense of entitlement rather than a need to perform.

Generation Y is also the most diverse generation ever (35 percent are non-white) and also the most tolerant, believing everyone should be part of the community.

Another Y Generation

Nancy Robinson, a research analyst at a consumer research company based in Minneapolis, Minnesota, has identified a subset of Generation Y, referred to as the YoCos.

YoCos (Young Cosmopolitans) primarily reside in urban areas and have an increasing disposable income. They are married to their work and are staying single by choice—at least for now. Some share the rent with roommates while others are living with their parents.

YoCos show a preference for convenience-driven and digital lifestyles, music and art, smart and hip products and services, and those that promise intense sensory experiences like extreme sports, action-filled adventure weekends, worldwide travel, and authentic ethnic foods. They seem especially open to a multicultural perspective.

"It's a growing group of Millennials partly because of the immediacy of technology and travel, but also the increasing culturalism of American youth," Robinson explained.

Generation Z *Born 1996-?*

Generation Z is one of the proposed names for the generation born after Generation Y. The New Silent Generation is another name used to refer to them, since some historians believe history will repeat itself, and they will share some of the same characteristics of the Silent Generation—the generation of their grandparents and great-grandparents.

Realistically, it's still too early to say how society will shape this generation, but experts predict they will be intellectual, confident, culturally-minded, and politically active.

Generation Z will be larger than Generation X (their parents) because of a trend towards rising birth rates, but they will still be far smaller, both in total numbers and per year count of births, than Generation Y.

Due to increasing health and medical advancements, this generation will likely have an extremely long life span. In 1950, the life expectancy of Americans was sixty-nine. Researchers now indicate that half of the North American babies born since 2000 will live to an age of ninety, and 10 percent to one hundred years of age.

Association experts are skeptical that membership associations will adapt and survive long enough to be present in the lives of Generation Z.

The following example demonstrates a way in which one association is making an effort to bridge the generation gap and ensure its future success.

NEW RECRUITS BRIDGE THE GENERATION GAP

U.S. Women of Today

Founded in 1985, the United States Women of Today encompasses sixteen states and has four thousand members. Despite their twenty-one-year history, Janet Esper, past president for the organization, states, "We're struggling to get up and going."

The organization has dreams of growing much larger, which is why it is encouraging each chapter to recruit at least one member a month—preferably a younger member.

"They are the foundation of our future; they will carry on the organization. If we don't recruit them, we'll be obsolete," Esper stated.

In an effort to meet the needs and interests of the younger age groups, Women of Today started offering scholarships for student members; introduced technology, public speaking, and leadership courses; revamped its membership manuals and simplified its forms; started relying solely on e-mail; and introduced a big sister mentoring program for new members.

The Women of Today also realized their organization's passion for community causes is shared by the younger generations. The organization is pushing each chapter to hone in on a local charity and let that charity be an identifying part of that chapter.

One cause that was adopted focused on the homeless. "We have a lot of young women coming in to volunteer. That helps out when you have an organization that younger members can identify with," Esper said.

She said Women of Today has realized the importance of fostering a relationship with younger members and inviting their involvement.

"My challenge to our community and other members is that we give them a chance to prove themselves. When they ask us to do something a different way, we need to give them the privilege of doing that. It's our way of getting them involved."

Questions to consider:

1. Which aspects of your association's offerings do the younger members use the most?

2. Which aspects do they use the least?

3. Visualize your association five years from now. What do you see?

4. Who do you see?

5. How has the association changed?

MISSION & MARKETING— WHAT'S IN IT FOR ME?

THREE

*"The best industry associations offer a lifeline to their members—be it accreditation, legal advice, access to resources, trade shows, business opportunities, industry news, or networking clubs.
But the worst will take their members' not-insubstantial subscriptions in exchange for a logo, a line in the directory, and a limp Christmas party. ...
Ask not what you can do for your association, but what it can do for you—demand value for money."*

—*Contract Journal*, Dec. 10, 2003

Today's workforce is working 130 extra hours per year. One-eighth of the workforce is caring for an aging relative and a child under the age of eighteen.

As a result, people desperately seek more balance in their lives, crave more personal time, and choose to withdraw from associations that fail to convey their membership benefits, worth, and value.

The last thing your members want is to waste their time attending long or numerous meetings, waiting in line at events, feeling pressured to buy or do something, or being inconvenienced in any way.

It's difficult for most membership associations to keep Baby Boomers involved and nearly impossible to recruit and retain the younger generations.

Generations X and Y are time-conscientious, career-driven, family-focused, globally-minded, and well-educated. And they hold drastically different life-experiences and expectations from their Baby Boomer and Traditional predecessors.

So, their questions to membership organizations will inevitably be: Why should I join? What's in it for *me*?

While other generations may be pondering the same questions, Generation X is the first generation to demand answers—and so far, few organizations have been able to respond to the Xers' satisfaction.

If membership associations are going to appeal to the younger generations, they must be able to think of themselves in a different way, which in many cases means a complete repositioning of the organization's mission and marketing efforts.

The myths and realities listed below will help you gain a better understanding of how Boomer-centric associations perceive New Recruits and what New Recruits really want.

Myth #1:

Younger generations are not joiners. They have little to no interest in joining membership organizations.

Reality:

Younger generations will join, if they are invited.

Membership associations can't just hand a New Recruit a membership application and expect it to be filled out. Likewise, associations who focus on fast-talking, aggressive sales strategies in place of relationship-building opportunities are making a serious mistake when it comes to recruiting younger members.

When it comes to recruiting and retaining younger members, the strategy of building value and relationships is imperative. Younger generations *are* joiners of membership organizations, as long as they are provided with a sense of belonging, given adequate opportunities to contribute, and their participation is valued.

Remember: The younger generations are savvy and skeptical consumers. Generation X and Y were raised with advertising and telemarketing, not to mention political scams and high divorce rates. As a result, they rely only on the people and organizations who take the time to establish a relationship with them and earn their trust.

They want to know that membership associations are concerned about their needs and interests and are actively engaged in developing programs and services especially for them.

Equate the recruiting process to a formal dinner party—without the fancy dresses and all the formalities, of course. Younger generations are not wallflowers. They like to be the life of the party. They want to be invited, properly introduced and served, given a seat at the head table, attended to throughout their meal, and given the opportunity to be in the spotlight.

You will soon discover that when you make a place for younger generations, they show up.

Myth #2:
Younger generations want networking opportunities.

Reality:
Younger generations want networking opportunities and much more.

Baby Boomers are social animals, very much a team generation. They like to do things in groups and are very comfortable in the presence of other people.

Actually, since the beginning of time, the desire to socialize in groups has been a core value of membership associations, and they often tout these plentiful networking opportunities to prospective members.

Here again, the New Recruits are changing history.

Generation X is a generation that tends to be very independent, individualistic, self-reliant, and often prefers to work alone. Generational consultant Chuck Underwood warns that association events "loaded with golf and cocktail hours and schmoozing" can be a real turn off to Gen X.

"Most associations are multi-generational environments, immersing Generation Xers into crowds comprised mostly of non-Xers. Yet Xers are very peer-focused," Underwood said.

The one exception to this rule is providing age-specific networking opportunities. As a result of the prevalent divorces and political scams that took place during their youth, Xers are skeptical of older generations, but they are comfortable networking with people their own age.

More so than networking opportunities, Generation X is looking for career-building opportunities from an association membership.

Generation Y is a little more socially outgoing than Gen X, but does rely heavily on technology to communicate with others. In addition to networking, Gen Y is looking for a way to make a difference in their community.

This generation has a broad worldview as a result of being raised with the Internet, more diversity in their schools, and the Peace Corps mentality of their parents. They would prefer to join a membership association where a portion of their dues support a cause or their involvement opportunities include community service projects and volunteerism.

Myth #3:
Younger generations are more concerned about preserving their personal time than building their careers.

Reality:

Younger generations want both.

USA Today labeled Gen X as the Family First Generation.

As the first generation of latchkey children raised in two working parent households, Generation X values their family and personal time more than anything else. This generation introduced the concept of balance to the workplace, and they want the flexibility to take care of their now-adult responsibilities–including children–better than their parents did.

Xers draw a very hard line between their work hours and their personal hours. They don't like obligations that are going to intrude on their non-work hours as association life might often request and require.

Nevertheless, Generation X also places a high value on professional development. Continually aware of being laid off or downsized, they remain focused on career security and aim to build a personal repertoire of skills and experience. Career seminars and workshops are always a big hit with Gen Xers.

Generation Y is also very career-oriented, claiming the largest number of business start-ups among college and high school students in history.

This generation is expected to change jobs seven times before they reach their early thirties. This is largely due to the fact that they were raised with a strong entrepreneurial bent, questioning corporate America much like their Gen X predecessors. Even when working for someone else, they are thinking: How can I do this better? Or how can I use this to start my own consultancy?

Pursuing an aggressive career path, Generation Y values the idea of networking, the exchange of information, and they understand the importance of relationships, whether personal or professional.

But this is also the generation that grew up in a mission-driven, multi-tasking, multimedia world. Their personal time is a rare commodity simply because they are usually juggling school, relationships, family, and career.

The best way for membership associations to reach Gen Y is to utilize technology to provide access to career development and virtual networking opportunities twenty-four hours a day, seven days a week.

Myth #4:
Younger generations are not interested in leadership or volunteer roles.

Reality:
Younger generations willingly lead and volunteer.

Membership associations often find themselves agonizing over the fact that they can't get the younger generations to take a leading role. They claim association leadership is comprised mostly of Baby Boomers simply because the New Recruits don't have any interest, are not reliable, and won't take the time.

The fact is younger generations are willing to lead and volunteer, but their expectations of both roles are quite different from that of their predecessors, starting with time management.

Boomer-centric associations are still abiding by Robert's Rules of Order and meeting for several hours several times a month. Younger generations detest the idea of long and numerous meetings. They view the process as a waste of their time and, therefore, resist taking on board or committee positions.

The New Recruits are willing to lead in situations where there is a no-nonsense meeting agenda intended for making decisions or delivering specific knowledge or training. They may also lead specific, one-time projects.

To expedite the decision-making process, associations need to use technology for some leadership discussion rather than relying solely on in-person meetings. Younger generations have a minimal need for face-to-face contact, which is the result of growing up with technology and in homes where both parents worked.

In addition to time management differences, participation differs from generation to generation, as well. Baby Boomers are likely to volunteer their services year after year simply because it's the right thing to do. The New Recruits won't volunteer, lead, or even join unless it's the right opportunity to pursue.

Due to their high regard for personal time, the participation of the New Recruits is likely to be episodic. They don't want to join an association and then work their way up the volunteer ranks as the previous generations did and as so many associations still expect. That takes too much time! They want to come in and do something that will benefit them, then that's it for a while.

Younger generations want a leading role in an association's leadership ranks. They will disengage from those things they feel powerless to influence. They are also not as likely to take an interest in tradition and will rebel against doing things the way they've always been done.

Remember: The Xers were raised to be self-sufficient, while the Yers were raised to be high-achievers. It's not that they disrespect tradition, but they do believe their insight and energy will positively influence an association and improve its way of serving members. (And they are right.)

To engage the participation of the New Recruits, associations must find ways to empower them, reward their kind of thinking, and recognize them for their contributions. For example, give them the opportunity to lead a committee or oversee a task, then reward them with a certificate or public recognition.

And once they do become actively involved, younger generations expect the experience to be a worthwhile, enjoyable experience. To the younger generations this equates to streamlined decision-making processes, information made available via technology, respectful use of their time, adequate reasons and opportunities to be personally involved, and plenty of fun.

Myth #5:

Younger generations do not take the time to read an association's marketing materials.

Reality:

Younger generations are heavily influenced by marketing materials.

Membership associations often make the mistake of thinking that their marketing materials use a one-size-fits-all approach, and that what works for the Boomers will work for the New Recruits, too.

Nothing could be further from the truth.

Raised on music videos and savvy television advertising, Generation X and Y have been pitched by marketers since infancy, and they have higher expectations and shorter attention spans when it comes to responding to marketing materials and sales pitches.

It takes only a few seconds to make a positive or negative impression—and that's especially true with the younger generations who are media-savvy consumers.

From Web sites to membership applications, membership associations need to seriously consider how they present themselves to the New Recruits to assure their messages are noticed, understood, persuasive, and meaningful to them. The New Recruits are quick to dismiss messaging that isn't on target, making it difficult for membership associations to regain their interest, much less their favor.

For the best results, use marketing messages that get to the point, are honest, incorporate member testimonials or stories, and highlight the benefits of membership and opportunities for participation. Don't use any fluff, hype, or sales strategies.

Don't use a three-fold brochure, either. Younger generations are savvy consumers who embrace sophisticated marketing messages that are visually-stimulating, innovative, concise, and professionally designed. Anything less struggles to get their attention. If your association is concerned about cost, craft a single message that addresses the needs and interests of each generation and alienates none.

Here's an example of effective marketing to multiple generations: A direct mail piece or Web page soliciting members by listing benefits with several bullet points of critical interest to each generation. Since Xers are looking for training to enhance their professional skill set, emphasize training in your bullet points. Since Boomers want networking opportunities, tell how your association provides those opportunities as well.

Phil Goodman, a generation researcher, takes this process a step farther. "You've got to remember: No generation follows another in mindset based upon the social circumstances they were raised with."

In other words, the experiences of each generation make them respond differently to certain words and images. Therefore, conduct focus groups to fully understand the lifestyles and values of the younger generations, and then craft messages specific to their interests and needs.

The same theory holds true for the recruiting and retention process. Associations have to develop messaging and processes specific to the needs and interests of younger generations. Associations have to gain their trust and prove a membership is valuable to their careers and relevant to their lives.

This means writing case studies that profile how memberships in your association have made a difference in your members' careers. It means elongating your recruiting process to allow more time for relationship-building, such as attending events together. *(More on this in chapter 8.)*

Bottom line: The myth is that recruiting and retaining younger members is an impossible challenge to overcome. The reality is that recruiting and retaining younger members is an undiscovered opportunity with great potential.

It's also your association's only succession plan.

Here are the stories of two historic associations changing their focus to recruit a new generation of members.

NEW RECRUITS
BRING A NEW PERSPECTIVE

Financial Women International (FWI)

FWI, founded in 1921, has always targeted mid-management and senior-level executives. For the first time in its history, the association recently shifted its focus to younger professionals.

"Presently, our average age member is near fifty, and we know that's close to retirement. We recognized that if we don't attract younger members, the eighty-year history of FWI will go away," stated Melissa Curzon, FWI board member.

As a result of FWI's discovery, the organization launched a student recruiting effort, featuring a membership discount and recruiting at job fairs and colleges; revamped its Web site; switched to electronic communication; introduced teleconferencing at the association's annual meeting; and created two levels of programming to appeal to both senior-level and entry-level professionals.

Despite all these changes, FWI still finds recruiting younger members a challenging task. "Because they've not been in the circle of knowing how associations can support their professional development, it's difficult for us to sell that concept until they've been in the workplace for a while and realize they need a safe place outside of work to talk," Curzon said.

Also, while older members look to their companies to support their involvement in FWI, younger members usually have to pay their own dues—largely due to the fact that company perks for entry-level employees are not as robust as they were in previous years.

Curzon said FWI's leadership has realized their new demographic is not afraid to share ideas and give feedback, and are more willing to volunteer on committees than sit on the board of directors. "They're juggling so many things that taking on a leadership position would come secondary to everything else. They want to get what they can get and move on," she said.

Nevertheless, Curzon said FWI is starting to observe a shift in its membership as more young women join the organization seeking mentorship and learning opportunities.

"We've had to re-imagine what FWI will look like with these new younger members, so we're hopeful it will prove to be an important resource for them [because] without them, FWI will go away."

Rotary Club of Chicago

The Rotary Club of Chicago was formed in 1905. (It is often referred to as Rotary One because it was the first Rotary Club and it was also the first organized service club.) According to Evy Alsaker of the Rotary Club of Chicago, the mission of the Rotary movement—service above self—has remained the same since its founding. It's the membership that has changed.

The Rotary Club of Chicago is still considered one of the larger clubs with two hundred members, but that is considerably lower than the seven hundred members the club previously boasted. Alsaker cited job transfers, busy work schedules, and travel as just a few of the reasons members are struggling to commit two to two-and-a-half hours every Tuesday for a meeting.

To help sustain the organization, Rotary Clubs have begun to aggressively recruit younger members, largely through community outreach.

For example, Early Act Club helps grade-school students identify and take responsibility for real-life problems within their school, local and global communities; Key Club involves Rotarians in service projects at area high schools; and RotorAct Club involves young professionals, ages eighteen to thirty, in service projects.

"We try to mentor people all along so that they can become regular Rotary members," Alsaker stated. "It's so important with the younger generations to get them actively involved right away. That ownership gives them a sense a purpose."

She said the Rotary organization has learned that younger generations want to be involved in service projects that correlate with their values, opportunities to gain leadership skills, and access to technology.

Alsaker believes Rotary will survive by continuing to seek out new ways and new generations to complete its original mission. "We need to continue what we've been building on for one hundred years and to continue to promote service above self and do things for others," she said. "We always have to address our mission."

Questions to consider:

1. What's the one value a membership in your association offers for Boomers? For Gen Xers? For Yers?

2. How are these values unique to your organization?

3. How are these values reason enough for people to want to pay annual dues, attend events, serve in leadership roles, and be actively involved in your organization?

4. Do these values meet the needs and interests of younger generations? Why or why not?

5. Does the way your association communicates meet the needs and interests of younger generations? Why or why not?

Here's an idea! *Reconsider your marketing and branding*

In the early 2000s, the average age of Minnesota Entrepreneurs' (ME) members was forty-five. The association implemented the following steps to increase the number of Gen X and Y memberships:

- Created a mission focused on inspiration, education, and networking, focusing on events that feature high-profile entrepreneurs (inspiration); panels of entrepreneurs who are experts on topics that target and interest members (education); and networking opportunities prior to each event;

- Restructured dues so members pay annual membership dues of $240, which include free admission to all ME events;

- Moved its events to a prestigious, trendy location in Minneapolis and upgraded the event amenities to appeal to younger professionals;

- Developed a feature-rich Web site and switched to all electronic communication;

- Started promoting the association and its events to four hundred editors in Minnesota and a one-thousand-person database;

- Charged board members with actively promoting the association;

- Advertised ME events with other associations and offered discounted admission prices to their members.

According to Dave Aasen of Minnesota Entrepreneurs, within three years of introducing these changes Minnesota Entrepreneurs experienced an influx of young professionals. The majority of the association's membership is now comprised of Gen X and Yers.

TECHNOLOGY AS NECESSITY

FOUR

FOUR

"I consider it a major accomplishment that I can work on a computer at age fifty—but they've grown up with technology, and they have an expectation that technology is going to support their effort."

- Susan Bowman, membership association consultant

An obvious generation gap exists when it comes to technology. Baby Boomers see technology as a revolutionary invention. Generation X finds technology useful, interesting, and important. Generation Y needs technology.

Generation Y has never known life without computers. The Digital Natives, as they are sometimes called, notably differ from the generations they succeed. As the Baby Boomers spent more time watching television than listening to the radio, so the Generation Yers spend more time on-line than watching television.

Technology as Necessity

Computers started popping up in workplaces and homes in the 1980s. Since then, technology evolved rapidly into a variety of mediums: Internet, e-mail, Instant Messaging, portable computers, cell phones, global positioning systems, portable digital media players, personal digital assistants, and more.

In the twenty-first century, most associations have a Web presence, but many still have not yet figured out how to use technology to their advantage.

Boomer-centric associations find themselves in a dilemma: While they want to make their technology as comfortable and friendly as a human transaction, they are concerned the technology will replace human interaction and the association will forever be altered.

New Recruit associations realize technology is the only way to sustain their membership.

After all, the younger generations were raised with technology, use it on a daily basis, and rely on it for everything from shopping to information-gathering to keeping in touch with friends and relatives. To them, technology is one of life's basic necessities.

There's just no way around it. Without adequate technology, associations will fail miserably in their efforts to reach younger members.

Web Sites and Virtual Communities

"When you look at associations' Web sites, they don't necessarily deliver technologically. They may have the content there, but it doesn't work from a technological advantage for them," stated Susan Bowman, association membership consultant.

What exactly is a technologically advanced Web site? For membership association purposes, it's a site that interests and engages younger generations, helps associations better manage their membership, and cuts costs in managing members.

Here's a list of must-haves for today's association Web sites:

- Content management system—Allows the association to add, edit, or delete any page on the site through a password protected area very easily, with very little technical know-how.

- On-line payments—Via secure credit card transaction pages, members can utilize the site to pay membership dues, register for programs and events, purchase merchandise, and make donations. Associations can easily track and process payments.

- Directory updates—Members can edit their contact information on-line, which helps keep the database current and accurate.

- Membership modules—There are dozens to choose from, including searchable membership directories, members-only section, discussion forums (blogs), frequently asked questions section, event calendar, news section for posting articles, newsletter archive, polls, and image galleries for posting photographs.
- Distance learning—Members can attend classes and take certification tests on-line.
- Streaming audio and video—Downloadable audio or video recordings, which allow members to access information shared at meetings, conferences, or special events.

"All of this improves value and benefit for an association," stated Mark Engel, an association Web services provider. While younger members are more likely to use and appreciate the technology, he said all ages are extremely satisfied when the information they need about the association and what it offers is available on-line.

Webinars, streaming audio and video, and distance learning opportunities are especially appealing to younger generations. When these time-pressed, career-driven, family-oriented generations can't attend a meeting, event, or class, the association can use these technologies to offer the experience to them in a downloadable format free or for a minimal fee.

Furthermore, membership associations should supplement their Web sites with electronic communication tactics, such as offering e-memberships, using HTML e-invites for programs and events, publishing e-newsletters, and moving to e-membership directories. Younger members are more likely to appreciate these formats.

Some of the most successful organizations have built communities on-line via expanded Web site offerings to interest younger members. Rather than attending an event, the younger generations prefer the virtual networking offered by blogs and on-line bulletin boards, where they share information and network on their own time at any hour on any day.

Nancy Robinson, Millennial research analyst, referred to Friendster (www.friendster.com) as an example of a meeting site that is popular with Generation Y.

"It used to be that this generation went online to set up virtual relationships and information share, but now they're using Friendster to set up monthly meetings on-line as a way to connect. Associations can look at this model, tweak it a bit, and put it in a package that lets this generation know the value of joining their friend circle," she said.

Blogging and Podcasting

Blogging and podcasting are widely used by people under the age of forty—the New Recruits—and are challenging associations to rethink the way they communicate with their younger audiences and build relationships.

A blog is an on-line version of a journal or diary. Blog comments are typically conversational, which encourages an exchange of views and insights on a particular topic. Because most blogs offer readers the opportunity to post comments, they provide an opportunity for two-way communication that implicitly tells Web users their input is valued.

Blogs also help improve a Web site's search engine performance, particularly if the content is relevant to your members and includes the keywords and phrases your prospects are searching for.

Shopfloor.org is a business blog hosted by the National Association of Manufacturers at http://blog.nam.org. Members discuss important issues affecting manufacturing, small businesses, free markets, outsourcing, energy prices, taxes, and staying competitive in the business world.

Another example of a blog is IABC Communications Commons, http://commons.iabc.com/, hosted by the International Association of Business Communicators. This blog features an ever-changing community of communicators who share their insights and expertise and engage in a dialogue with readers.

The New Recruits, especially Gen Y, use blogs for information-gathering. As a generation that grew up using technology, blogging to them is the equivalent of having a telephone conversation—it's an efficient and rewarding exchange of information.

While blogging is text-driven, podcasting is the on-line adaptation of broadcasting a radio or television show. Podcasting distributes audio or video over the Internet, which can be downloaded for playback on mobile devices and personal computers.

Associations can use podcasting to present information about a relevant topic, feature interviews with members or association staff, or excerpts from an event or seminar.

For example, the American Institute of Architects hosts *Architecture Knowledge Review*, a podcast series for design professionals featuring interviews with architects and other design professionals.

The American Heart Association podcast delivers free audio reports to keep the public updated on new ways to reduce disability and death from cardiovascular disease and stroke.

According to the Association Community Blogs and Podcasts, a master list of associations using blogs and podcasts, in 2006 there are twenty-five associations on record as having blogs and eleven associations on record as using podcasts.

Associations have yet to discover that these technologies can help them connect with younger members and reintroduce some of the productive relationships of previous years; the kind of relationships that membership associations fostered at networking socials and annual conferences during the 1980s and 1990s.

Here are just a few of the ways membership associations can utilize blogs and podcasts to their advantage:

- **Create an RSS feed of your press releases.** (RSS stands for Really Simple Syndication, a form of Web syndication used by news Web sites and blogs.) Open up a rapid distribution mechanism to bloggers and reporters who prefer to get information via RSS. RSS is the next iteration of the traditional blast fax or e-mail, and it covers more territory, opening up your association to more publicity opportunities.

- **Launch a monthly podcast series with your association president or a rotating roster of key executives to share your knowledge on the state of the industry.** Send out e-mails to your member database to solicit questions or topics in advance.

- **Start a focused public blog.** Blog about a specific issue that is important to your association or innovations in your industry. Find someone in your association who has a distinct voice and passion and give them tools that allow them to effectively advocate for your industry.

- **Start a members' only blog on your intranet/extranet.** Use it as a tool to report back to your members on your association activities and engage their feedback and participation.

The Future

Technology changes so rapidly it can be difficult to predict its future. Obviously, the generational shift will continue to spur significant changes, and it's starting with the transition to community-building software.

Associations have relied on Association Management Systems, enterprise-wide software, for the past thirty years. In 2006, there is a movement away from this traditional software to customer relationship management as a result of the preferences of the younger generations.

"This idea of one-to-one marketing and one-to-one relationships—a lot of the association software wasn't designed for that," noted Reggie Henry, chief technology officer for the American Society of Association Executives.

Customer relationship management (CRM) is a holistic strategy that focuses on creating and maintaining lasting relationships with members. Watch for CRM software packages that help your association:

- Track critical information about each member, including services used, events attended, and products purchased;

- Develop personalized member service programs;
- Link members with special interest groups and discussions;
- Manage dues reports and association finances; and
- Complete event registration, fundraising activities, and marketing campaigns.

Furthermore, associations will likely invest in community and collaboration software, which will help them create virtual offices and committees, introduce Web conferencing capabilities, and create and deliver on-line professional development courses and multi-day on-line conferences.

What's the best way an association can implement technology? Ask for help. Ask the younger generation about their technological needs and wants, and then engage them in the actual development of the technology.

Too many associations have taken on a parent/child relationship and just assume the association leadership knows what is best for the younger members.

Give the New Recruits an opportunity to take the lead on technology. They are the Digital Natives, after all.

Technology defined

Blog—Also known as a Web log, a blog is a Web site in which comments are posted on a regular basis and displayed in reverse chronological order. Comments are written in a conversational style of documentation, usually focus on a particular topic of interest, and are comprised of text, images, and links to other Web pages, video, audio files.

Customer Relationship Management—CRM is the phrase used to describe either the software or the whole business strategy oriented on customer needs. CRM attempts to integrate and automate the various customer serving processes, personal information gathering and processing, and self-service within an organization.

iPod—This is a popular portable audio player designed and marketed by Apple Computer. The standard model stores media on a built-in hard drive. Like most digital audio players, an iPod can serve as an external data storage device when connected to a computer.

MP3—This is a digital audio player device which stores, organizes, and plays digital music files. MP3 can be used to play both audio CDs and homemade data CDs containing MP3 or other digital audio files.

Podcasting—This is a method of publishing audio or programs via the Internet, using syndication feeds for playback on mobile devises and personal computers. The result is a self-produced radio or television show.

RSS—This is an acronym for the Really Simple Syndication Web feed format. RSS feeds are used by the blogging community to share the latest entries' headlines or their full text and attached multimedia files. Available on any computer with Web access or via search engines for web feed content.

Streaming media—Media (audio or video) that is consumed (read, heard, viewed) while it is being delivered over computer networks.

Webinar—A seminar that is conducted over the Web and designed to be interactive between the presenter and audience. The presenter speaks over a standard telephone line, pointing out information being presented on screen, and the audience can respond over their own telephones.

NEW RECRUITS USE TECHNOLOGY TO DELIVER MEMBER BENEFITS

Association Forum of Chicagoland

In the association world, one of podcasting's earliest adopters is Association Forum of Chicagoland. On September 6, 2005, it began offering podcasts of its CEO column in *This Week@AssociationForum,* an on-line newsletter.

A podcast uses a feeder application—the best-known being RSS—to deliver new podcasts to subscribers as soon as they're posted on the Web. Listeners can also find new podcasts of interest by visiting aggregators—sites that continuously search for and capture podcasts, compile them into categories, and help users find and download information in their areas of interest.

You don't have to own an Apple iPod or any other kind of MP3 player to listen to a podcast. You can play the podcast on a computer, or burn it to a CD to listen to in cars, airplanes, or elsewhere.

Association Forum's podcasts are free to listeners. To create the podcasts, the association made an initial investment of less than $2,000 in hardware and software.

The Forum's 33,000 members are Chicago-area association executives on the lookout for new ways to serve their members. Accordingly, CEO Gary LaBranche lists the following three goals:

1. To demonstrate podcasting as an association product or service.

2. To share lessons about podcasting with the association community.

3. To provide more access to knowledge of association management.

LaBranche has found podcasting to be a quick and easy way to distribute information. "Dozens of Forum members have thanked us for demonstrating the technology," he said. "Younger members in particular have been very appreciative. As one said, 'I am part of the iPod generation, and the Forum's podcast effort speaks to me in a way that no other association has.' "

LaBranche predicts that podcasting will be "increasingly embraced by our ever-more-mobile society. It may well become a viable alternative to e-newsletters and other brief communication efforts."

Eventually, the Forum plans to allow members to listen to podcasts of articles from its magazine, interviews with authors and speakers, executive summaries of educational programs, and more.

Questions to consider:

1. When was the last time your organization introduced new technology to its members?

2. Which pages on your site generate the most traffic and which generate the least?

3. What is your technology budget? How do you determine if your budget is adequate?

4. Are you still a paper-based organization, relying mostly on print materials to communicate with your members? If so, how much do these print materials cost to produce on an annual basis?

5. How can your association use technology to engage younger members, bring value, and enhance the overall membership experience?

STUDENTS COUNT

"All of us in the profession feel a sense to make the profession stronger and better when we leave it than when we entered it. We want to have the new thinkers in. It's inevitable that organizations should always be prepared for changing of the guard and bringing in new ideas."

—Lorraine Koc, National Association of Women Lawyers

For the Boomer-centric association, college students are last on their list of membership recruits. These associations are overly concerned about building their membership of dues-paying professionals.

The New Recruit association places student recruitment high on its list of priorities—college students, high school students, and even younger. These associations have a succession plan in mind, and tend to generate more memberships in the long run.

Consider this: If students don't need your association in college, during their formative years of preparation for a profession and personal development, why would they have a need for your association later on in life?

A number of ways to recruit students exist, including the formation of student chapters, forming alliances with local universities or colleges, offering mentoring programs, providing discounted memberships, or hosting job fairs and other events geared towards students.

First and foremost, association leaders must engage students in the planning and development of a student initiative. Don't assume that the Baby Boomers know what's best for the students. Give the students an opportunity to lead, and your association will be more likely to succeed.

For example, in working with the students, association leaders will soon learn the traditional format of a student chapter with a board of directors and regularly scheduled meetings is a turn off for most Gen Yers. Associations are now challenged to think of student chapter development more as a community where students go for resources or support, and the best resource for that information is the students themselves.

Furthermore, in working with the students, association leaders can expect to learn that the two most successful student recruiting tools for Generation Y are mentoring programs and Webinars.

Mentoring programs, whether set up for face-to-face interaction or as e-mentoring via e-mail, give Gen Y the opportunity to be matched with a professional they can respect and rely on for advice.

Webinars give Gen Y the flexibility they need to attend classes and the opportunity they want to connect with an association when it's convenient for them.

Here are some additional tips for effective student recruitment:

1. **Read your materials from their vantage point.** Your association's standard professional membership benefits probably won't work with students. Remember, they are still in school or new to the workplace. They don't have the money, time, or clout to attend meetings, publish in journals, or volunteer. Consider what's really important to them and ways to market those benefits to them.

2. **Talk about your membership benefits, not features.** Features are what your organization does; benefits are the personal connection for members. Don't just say, "We have a career center." Instead announce, "We have a career center that helps you find your way in the world of work. You can find helpful tips on how to talk with supervisors and how to get through that first job evaluation."

3. **Set up the offer.** When students participate in conferences or events, let them

know you have a great offer to convert them to professional members, and explain why membership is so important as they start their new career.

4. **Encourage students to keep in touch.** In every communication, let students know how they can update their records. Consider creating an e-mail address, such as studentname@yourassociation.org, so you can keep track of transitioning students.

5. **Offer connections.** Are students moving to a certain area? Provide their names to your members who work in that area and help them establish internships or mentoring opportunities.

6. **Be service-oriented.** During their first two years of membership, nurture students by contacting them frequently to be certain they receive information that helps them continue to answer the question, "What's in it for me to belong to this membership organization?" Develop and e-mail a tip-of-the-month message or a CD or DVD that's brief and focused on students. Blend entertainment and knowledge and let them know they are appreciated.

Responding to a need

More often than not, membership associations look to students to fulfill an unmet need within their organization or industry.

The first student chapter of Business and Professional Women (BPW) in the nation was chartered in April 2003, in Springfield, Missouri, on the campus of Southwest Missouri State University. Development of the SMSU student chapter was spearheaded by members of the Greater Ozarks Business and Professional Women's organization.

BPW immediately realized the need for its student chapters to be student-driven. "The students have their own special needs and interests because they're developing their careers and have special interests," said Debora Biggs, past president of the Missouri Business and Professional Women's Federation. "So we found some good students on campus who were enthused about doing it, and they promoted it through campus avenues."

While the start-up phase proved difficult on the university campus, once students became familiarized with BPW, it became much easier to establish relationships with them.

BPW has experienced the same success with its Young Careerist (YC) program. For the past forty years, YC engaged young women in a speaking competition. The competition is initiated on a local level, followed by state and national competitions.

"Because the program is only open to those women ages 21-30, we have gained younger members and a younger perspective through the program," noted Tricia Fleisher Fadness, BPW USA. As a result of the competition, many YC participants get exposed to BPW for the first time, and end up liking the experience and become actively involved.

Biggs said BPW enjoys the advantage of being an organization with a variety of women in different occupations, which brings tremendous networking and professional opportunities for students.

The National Kitchen and Bath Association (NKBA) has already experienced the rapid growth in student chapters that BPW envisions for itself.

In 2004, NKBA had five student chapters. A year later, the association boasted fifteen student chapters and a goal to establish forty-five chapters by 2010.

Why the rush?

According to Tracy Hawkins of NKBA, the association foresees student outreach as one of the most effective ways to resolve an industry-wide worker shortage.

Student recruitment has become one of the most important tasks the NKBA has identified for itself in an effort to resolve the worker shortage through education and mentoring opportunities. The association is dedicating a considerable amount of time and resources to developing student chapters nationwide.

The New Recruit

NKBA has 30,000 members in the United States and Canada; 1,500 who are students. Students pay $15 a year to be members. Dues for industry members range from $150 to $9,500 based on gross annual business revenue.

Recruitment efforts have been very successful for NKBA, which launched a recruiting and marketing campaign in 2005 to interior design schools nationwide. Hawkins said NKBA's success in attracting students is due in part to networking opportunities, but primarily students join for its unique career development opportunities and expansive membership benefits, such as professional development courses, industry certifications, and free admission to industry trade shows.

NKBA requires its student members to obtain an internship to prepare them for the transition to the workforce. "Many students get a job from that internship, or they make so many connections that they get a job right out of school," Hawkins said.

NKBA distributes a student e-newsletter four times a year; offers student pricing for courses, books, trade shows, and planning software; and hosts a members-only student Web site featuring a message board, resume post, and a list of scholarships and design competitions.

Hawkins equated student chapters to other associations that use special interest groups, stating, "When you find that those interest groups are significant, you're certainly going to address their needs and encourage them to participate and strengthen the organization as a result."

NEW RECRUITS FOSTER RELATIONSHIPS WITH STUDENTS

BizLounge Network

BizLounge Network is a dues-paying organization established in 2000 to foster entrepreneurship in the Minneapolis-St. Paul area. The membership is comprised of students and young professionals who own a business or have a business idea and need help getting started.

The founders of BizLounge realized these young entrepreneurs needed an environment to exchange ideas, educate each other, and have some fun—so the organization was created to address their unique preferences. All communication takes place through the Web site or virtual tools, and meetings are held at local restaurants or businesses.

Since the beginning, one of the organization's main goals has been focused on providing mentoring opportunities to college undergraduates. BizLounge immediately established connections with entrepreneurship programs at area colleges and universities and developed a mentoring program.

"We wanted to position ourselves to combine efforts with some of the schools, because those are the places you're going to find those that need that extra push to start that business," said Joe Keeley, BizLounge director.

The mentorship program involves individuals who own companies with $1 million in sales or more, mentoring those who have $500,000 to $1 million in sales. The mentoring program is helping BizLounge achieve its goal of fostering entrepreneurship in the Twin Cities, as well as bringing in a constant stream of new members.

"We strive to create a win-win scenario by creating a mentoring environment that fosters relationships between business students and seasoned entrepreneurs. Students create relationships that enable a smoother transition from campus to starting their business, while entrepreneurs benefit from the fresh perspectives and talents of the students," Keeley said.

National Association of Women Lawyers

The National Association of Women Lawyers (NAWL) is one of the oldest bar associations in the United States, originally founded in the late 1890s.

For students, the organization hosts a law school writing competition, presents an annual law student award, and offers a program focused on professional development.

"We are trying to recruit younger attorneys through one device called Backpack to Briefcase, a program that we've done in several cities for law students, to give them some advice on what the issues will be when they go into a law firm," explained Lorraine Koc of NAWL.

Backpack to Briefcase was originally hosted in law firms, but NAWL quickly realized the flaw in that plan. "We had a 50 percent no-show rate, and we believe it was because we were not on campus. Law students had to pre-register, then on Friday didn't feel like getting dressed or going downtown," Koc said.

Since NAWL made the move to bring the program to the students, Backpack to Briefcase has been well-attended and received rave reviews from students.

The initial goal of the program was to give law students advice on topics like time management, appropriate dress, presentation skills, and working with other partners in the firm, but NAWL is now hoping Backpack to Briefcase will assist the organization with its membership recruiting efforts.

"We started to think about that pipeline issue," Koc stated, referring to the need to get younger generations involved in NAWL to prepare for succession planning. "I wish we had been smarter in thinking about it sooner."

Questions to consider:

Does your association offer programs, services, or benefits to students?

- If so, what plans does your association have for expanding its reach and involving more students?

- If not, what are two actions your association can take within the next month to get a student membership program started?

Here's an Idea! *Job Shadowing*

The University of Texas-Austin is home to a student chapter of the Austin Association for Women in Communications, which has thirty-five student members. The chapter has had the most success targeting first-year students entering the communications school.

"A major selling point for our organization is called Shadow Day, where one day every semester we pair students with professionals in the career of their choice, and they job shadow that person for the day," said Amy Casteen of AWC.

The chapter also offers a semester-long mentoring program in which students and professionals are paired up and engage in a relationship through e-mail, over scheduled coffees or lunches, or by attending the professional chapter meetings and other industry events together.

The mentoring and job shadowing programs have been the chapter's most successful endeavors. The chapter also invites students to serve on the board of directors. Casteen said this has become an effective selling point when it comes to recruiting prospective students.

THE YP
MOVEMENT

"Truth is, my generation—Gen X—doesn't join Rotary, and we wouldn't be caught dead singing 'My Bonnie Lies Over the Ocean.' But that doesn't mean we don't have our own gig going. Today, young professionals are showing up, reaching out, and digging in through young professional networks."

—Rebecca Ryan, generation consultant

While membership associations were struggling to understand the generation gap, the younger generation became annoyed and frustrated and decided to form their own membership association.

Young professional (YP) organizations are the New Recruit's membership association, and they're popping up throughout the United States and beyond.

There are currently ninety active YP networks across the country, many of which boast thousands of members. If that's not a wake-up call for the membership associations still stuck in Boomerland, then nothing will be.

What makes YP associations different from other membership associations? In addition to the age differences, YP associations are:

- Media savvy and actively promote their organizations;
- Inventing new and faster ways to do things themselves rather than relying on traditional power structures;
- Focusing on making a positive contribution within their communities; and
- Measuring their success (income and expense ratios, perception changes, retention indicators) to make their case as viable, competitive associations.

Younger members love the YP model because it responds to their interests and needs as young professionals. It recognizes that Gen Xers and Yers don't want to join associations to attend long and numerous meetings. They want to be empowered as positive forces for change.

YP organizations have been very influential on their respective communities, even going so far as to boost the local economy.

For example, since its inception in 2001, Metropolitan Milwaukee Association of Commerce's Young Professionals of Milwaukee (YPM) has grown to more than four thousand members and serves as an important attraction and retention initiative for the Milwaukee business and non-profit community.

In 2000, Milwaukee's population had fallen from the twenty-fourth largest city-region to forty-third. Metropolitan Milwaukee Association of Commerce founded YPM to work with city and regional officials on an economic development initiative with the belief that a city influenced by young professionals is a city that can attract and retain young professionals.

YPM gives its members access to the people, places, and initiatives that are unique to Milwaukee; connects members with emerging leader service opportunities; welcomes newcomers and student interns to the city; and keeps its members current on urban developments and key community issues.

YPM has managed to attract a large membership base for four main reasons:

1. **A worthwhile call to action.** YPM's role is to shape and showcase a Greater Milwaukee that is more attractive to diverse young talent. It's a serious role with measurable and significant outcomes. The New Recruits want to give back to their communities, and they want to know that their time will be well spent doing something that makes a difference. An opportunity like

this differs considerably from a social club or sales leads exchange group.

2. **Real member benefits.** YPM provides its members with unique opportunities, such as access to city officials, exclusive information on city happenings, and opportunities to experience featured art performances and Milwaukee's best restaurants.

3. **Numerous involvement opportunities.** From the on-line posting service that connects members with non-profit mentoring, board leadership, fund raising, and other service opportunities to community events and volunteer opportunities, there are several quick and easy ways to get involved and feel a sense of belonging.

4. **Affordable pricing.** YPM members attend events for $15 or less. Annual dues are $50.

"If you're fifty years old and vice president of a company, you can join a chamber of commerce. If you're twenty or thirty years old, you're not likely to join the chamber or attend $200 dinners to be social or a $25 breakfast. It's not something our age group is going to do," stated F. Anne Harrel, founder of the Boston Young Professionals Association (BYPA).

BYPA and YPM are modeled much the same. BYPA's membership is $35 per year, which includes admission to weekly networking events.

BYPA hosts a variety of social and networking events, and professional and personal development seminars. Like YPM, BYPA focuses on a community perspective. Instead of economic development, however, BYPA focuses on charity benefits and volunteering.

In many ways, YP associations are a kickback to the social activism prevalent in the 1960s and 1970s. That's really no surprise, considering that the parents of Gen Xers and Gen Yers experienced that era and likely passed on their values to their children.

The Jaycees

And what about the Jaycees? This association has been targeting young professionals, ages eighteen to forty, since 1915. Undoubtedly, this association was the first young professionals association in America.

The Jaycees experienced the greatest amount of growth between the 1940s and 1970s. Membership has declined since 2000, partly due to the fact that Jaycees strayed from their original mission of leadership development to focus on community service initiatives.

Within the scope of community service, there are many competitors—from the Red Cross to the up-and-coming YP groups. The Jaycees executive team realized they needed to refocus and hold steadfast to their original mission of developing leaders.

In the meantime, even the Jaycees have been surprised by the generational shift that's taken place. Because

Jaycees have to retire their memberships by the time they turn forty, this association has already observed the passage of the Boomers.

"There's a huge difference today between an eighteen-year-old and a forty-year-old," noted Lars Hajslund of the International Jaycees, referring to the use of technology. "There's more of a difference now than there was in the 1950s and 1960s."

The Jaycee leaders don't foresee young professional groups threatening their existence, but by the same token the Jaycees are growing at a much slower pace than YP groups.

The YP Difference

The phrase "if you can't beat them, join them" comes to mind when I think of YP groups.

The Boomer-centric association is likely to believe that the formation of young professional groups aren't essential and will develop a half-hearted recruiting effort to interest younger members.

The New Recruit association will do everything in its power to form an innovative, successful young professional's initiative and showcase it throughout its membership and marketing efforts.

In either case, the evidence is clear that YP associations—whether founded by an existing association or developed as an independent entity—are successful. Really successful.

The New Recruit

There are few associations that can claim ten thousand members within one city's limits—but BYPA can.

There are few associations that can recruit four thousand new members in less than five years—but YPM did.

Tulsa's Young Professionals was introduced in March 2005 by the Tulsa Metro Chamber of Commerce. Within a few months, the organization had grown to one thousand members.

The City Club of Cleveland, Greater Sarasota Chamber of Commerce, Risk Management Association, Chamber of Commerce of Fargo-Moorhead, American Medical Association, and many other associations have similar stories to share.

Is this mere coincidence? I don't think so.

NEW RECRUITS FIND A PLACE IN YP GROUPS

Fargo-Moorhead Young Professionals Network

The Chamber of Commerce of Fargo-Moorhead introduced a Young Professionals Network (YPN) in 2004 to respond to the needs and interests of younger members and actively engage them in the chamber. In less than two years, YPN had 260 new members.

"We wanted to bring younger members into the organization to create that future base. But also, we were hearing from younger people that they wanted a forum that was not intimidating because of the older professionals in the organization," said Nicole Paczkowski of YPN.

"One of our best attended events was when we pulled together commissioners and city council members to talk about how younger people could get involved in committees and serve on boards. We made them go around from table to table to introduce themselves so they made valuable connections with our members," Paczkowski said.

YPN organized a similar event with local media professionals.

"We've experienced incredible success, but know that we have to continue offering quality programming in order to grow," Paczkowski said. The organization has engaged in talks with other YPs in hopes of growing a regional network and offering more opportunities for its membership.

TwinWest Chamber of Commerce, Minnetonka, Minnesota

In 2001, TwinWest Chamber of Commerce grabbed the attention of its Generation X and Y members by launching a group called Emerging Leaders. Members responded enthusiastically, and more than two hundred members joined within the first three years.

One particularly popular event is after-hours speed networking. Thirty Emerging Leaders come together to exchange business cards and promote their companies in forty-five second commercials. These sessions usually sell out.

Another successful program is the Lunch with Leaders series, featuring a luncheon with an accomplished business leader or community figure. After the luncheon, the group is afforded private access to the leaders to ask questions and share ideas.

The Emerging Leaders are also committed to the community. Every month, they take a crew of four to six young professionals to a crisis childcare center to cook dinner for the children.

"The Emerging Leaders' mission of networking and creating effective business professionals is also their secret to growth: They convince colleagues and friends of the value in Emerging Leaders and the TwinWest Chamber," stated Barb Obershaw, president. "They love being a part of this active, progressive group, and as a result TwinWest continues to recruit and retain young members."

Greater Waco Chamber of Commerce Young Professionals Committee

Waco, Texas, is a college town, and when the Greater Waco Chamber of Commerce leaders recognized the college students were leaving town after graduation and coming back in their mid-thirties, they realized the need to maintain the community workforce and resolve the generation gap.

The Chamber also realized the city's need to overcome a traumatic past, marred by the Branch Davidian incident.

"The young people were tired of this negative image that Waco was portraying. The young people wanted to do something about that and show that we're bigger than that," explained Stacey Maness, economic development director for the Chamber.

As a result, the Young Professionals Committee was established by the Chamber to promote Waco's quality of life and to attract and retain a labor force of educated twenty-five to thirty-five-year-olds.

The group is working to accomplish this goal by encouraging companies to hire new graduates, promoting Waco's opportunities to college students, hosting social events for young professionals, and educating the business community on the value of young professionals and the best practices in hiring and retaining them.

"The heart of our committees is research and development. We visit different cities to do research on what they have done to attract young professionals, and talk to different developers to find out how developments like that would fit into Waco's economy and demographics," Maness stated.

Since the development of YP, young people have become motivated to get the word out that Waco is a growing city, which has spurred enthusiasm, pride, and business growth.

"It's amazing how many people you can get on board when you just give them a venue to get moving and something that they're passionate about," Maness stated. "The young professionals needed a venue to get their thoughts across, and a separate committee was needed for that. They don't want to get lost in the chamber membership. The YPs can feel intimidated by that."

Questions to consider:

Does your association offer programs, services, or benefits to young professionals?

- If so, does your association have a plan for expanding its reach and involving more young professionals?

- If not, what are two actions your association can take within the next month to get a young professionals program started?

Here's an idea! *Provide more for less*

The PRSA-San Francisco chapter launched a Young Professionals group in 2003 to provide targeted educational programs for entry-level and junior-level PR practitioners and a forum where they can meet socially and network with each other.

The group's low-cost, bi-monthly programs are hosted by local PR departments of corporations and PR agencies. There, top PR executives provide attendees with tools and tips they can use to rise above their peers in media relations, writing, time management, and other skills aspiring PR practitioners need to develop early on.

The annual YP membership fee is $50, which is a cost-effective alternative to paying for events individually, and includes the value-added offerings listed below:

- Free admission to all YP educational programs and discounted admission to all YP social mixers;
- Access to job listings on PRSA-San Francisco's Web site, currently available to members only;
- Discounted admission rate to PRSA professional development and regular programs;
- Discounted PRSA chapter membership upon time of transitioning from YP membership;

- The opportunity to serve on YP or other chapter committees; and
- Access to PRSA-San Francisco's monthly electronic newsletter.

BUDGET

SEVEN

"I have not seen anybody who's making money on their students and young professionals, but they are thinking that in the long-term it's really the best way to go for getting people engaged in their association. And realistically, you're not making all the money on the membership dues. You make it on the purchases down the road."

—Carylanne Pishner,
American Society of Association Executives

Is your organization afraid to spend money on recruiting?

The Boomer-centric organization will constantly worry about spending money to recruit new members. Its leadership will either maintain a one-size-fits-all mentality and strongly oppose the need to customize its recruiting efforts according to age or other demographics, or will take what I refer to as the recliner approach, maintaining a status quo position of sitting back and waiting for new members to find them.

The New Recruit organization knows it will have to spend money now if it wants to make money later. Its leadership is planning ahead, realizing that sooner or later the failure to recruit and retain younger members will diminish the association's bottom line.

But how does an organization start the recruiting process? How does it know what to do and how much money to budget?

Association Analysis

The creation of a new, aggressive recruiting program requires a strategic approach. The first step is to analyze all of the association's existing programs, services, and member benefits and methods of communication and compare them to the values and interests of the New Recruits.

In the chart below, list all of your association's current offerings in their respective categories. Then, for each offering listed, place a checkmark in the boxes that follow to positively indicate if that offering uses technology, offers a tangible or measurable benefit, provides a professional development opportunity, includes a community service component, requires a time commitment of fewer than two hours per month, and costs less than $30 per month.

The New Recruit

Association offerings	Uses technology	Tangible or measurable	Professional development	Community service	Fewer than 2 hrs/mo	Less than $30/mo
Programs & Events						
1.						
2.						
3.						
4.						
5.						
6.						
7.						
8.						
Services & Benefits						
1.						
2.						
3.						
4.						
5.						
6.						
7.						
8.						
Communications						
1.						
2.						
3.						
4.						
5.						
6.						
7.						
8.						

Budget

Association offerings	Uses technology	Tangible or measurable	Professional development	Community service	Fewer than 2 hrs/mo	Less than $30/mo
Volunteer/Involvement Opportunities						
1.						
2.						
3.						
4.						
5.						
6.						
7.						
8.						
Other						
1.						
2.						
3.						
4.						
5.						
6.						
7.						
8.						

If your checkmarks are plentiful and evenly distributed throughout the document, then you're well on your way to becoming an association that's focused on the New Recruit.

If your checkmarks are few and far between, your association is still Boomer-centric and needs to expand its offerings to appeal to younger members.

In either case, you can now see for yourself where your organization is making strides to appeal to younger members and where it needs extra help.

Needs and Cost Assessment

The next step is to highlight those areas that need extra help and list the ways in which your association could potentially introduce new offerings and benefits to appeal to the New Recruits.

In the chart on the next page, list all the offerings from the chart on previous two pages with fewer than three checkmarks next to them. These are areas of focus for your association. Expanding these offerings to interest younger members will simplify the recruiting process.

Next to each area of focus, write down ways your association can expand or restructure the offering to effectively interest New Recruits. Take into consideration the checkpoints from above: uses technology, offers a tangible or measurable benefit, provides a professional development opportunity, includes a community service component, requires a time commitment of fewer than two hours per month, and costs less than $30 per month.

In the last column, assign a ballpark estimate of how much each change will cost the association.

Budget

Areas of Focus	Ways to Restructure to Appeal to the New Recruits	Estimated Costs
Programs & Events • • • •		
Services & Benefits • • • •		
Communications • • • •		
Volunteer/Involvement Opportunities • • • •		
Other • • • •		

Now that you have a plan of action and related costs identified, your association can move forward with implementation and recruiting.

In addition, I recommend the following tactics for quickly and effectively recruiting younger members: Introduce a new dues category and new technology. These tactics are likely to burden your association's budget in the beginning, but in the long run they are great investments.

New Dues

Membership drops usually occur somewhere between student status and established professional status five to ten years after graduation from college. This is due to the fact that many associations have established student membership rates, but few have established young professional rates. Upon graduation from college, members are immediately bumped up to the full membership rate and the cost increase is more than most recent graduates can bear.

Think about it: As a young professional your bills for college are outstanding, you have an entry-level salary, and the company you're working for is not likely to pay your association dues until you have proven yourself.

To retain those student memberships and recruit more young professionals, offer a membership that is half or three-fourths less than the full membership rate for young professionals under the age of thirty.

The Boomer-centric association will panic at the thought of lowering dues because it has negative budget implications.

The New Recruit association, on the other hand, is willing to take a budgeting loss on the dues to engage and grow a young professional within the association. For this association, the long-term benefits outweigh the short-term risks.

The New Recruit association also realizes that more members joining at a lower rate offers more long-term growth potential for the association in comparison to a few members joining at a higher rate.

Carylanne Pishner, director of membership for the American Society of Association Executives, said young professionals and their employers refused to pay the $245 member rate. But when ASAE offered a $100 young professionals rate, two hundred members joined within six weeks.

New Technology

Business and real estate professionals use the phrase "location, location, location" to stress the importance of your whereabouts and how that inevitably affects your success, lifestyle, and emotional well-being.

Likewise, associations need to adopt the phrase "technology, technology, technology" to remind themselves that technology is the be-all, end-all vehicle that will inevitably affect their success and overall well-being.

In chapter 4, we learned the New Recruit uses technology, wants technology, and expects associations to offer technology. From a budgeting standpoint, this is by far the biggest investment associations will have to make to sustain the interests of younger members.

An association needs to consider the following costs when developing and maintaining its technology:

- Staff
- Infrastructure
- Hardware
- Software
- Professional Development
- Upkeep and Upgrades
- Web Design
- Electronic Mail Design (e-newsletters, e-invites, etc.)
- Web Hosting

First and foremost, invest in maintenance. Many associations, regardless of size, try to cut corners (i.e., cost) when it comes to technology. They resort to do-it-yourself techniques that can prove to be quite costly and risky overall.

For example, an association executive understands that keeping the workstations up-to-date with security patches, firewalls, anti-virus protection, and a back-up process will ward off the danger of hackers and nasty viruses. However, setting up these measures takes time and expertise that many executives feel their associations cannot afford.

The fact of the matter is your association *must* afford this protection. Small failures can be catastrophic for a membership association. Keep in mind that recovering from one malicious virus or having your association's Web site compromised by a hacker will cost more than any protective strategy.

I worked for a membership association that fell victim to a hacker. The hacker not only had access to employee information, but also hacked into the association's media database and sent out an announcement to local media in an effort to sabotage the association.

The event wreaked havoc on the association and all its employees for several weeks—something that could have easily been prevented with the proper time and resources dedicated to protecting its technology.

Less detrimental, but still a threat to be taken seriously, is the development of a Web site that isn't updated on a regular basis. You have to remember that younger generations spend more time on-line than watching television or engaging in most other recreational activities. They have zero tolerance for outdated information and will quickly disregard the association's credibility.

I recently came across an association's Web site, which noted in the same paragraph that it was founded in 1920 and that for the past seventy-nine years it has been a force for good in America and around the world.

The year I'm writing this book is 2006, and 1920 plus seventy-nine years equals 1999. That would imply that this association's Web site is seven years out of date!

You wouldn't purchase a billboard on Main Street with information about your association that was outdated, and your Web site shouldn't be any different. For the New Recruits, the Web is the first place they go for information. So if your association can't afford all the bells and whistles, at least hire someone to maintain the Web site on a weekly—if not daily—basis.

On the flip side, there is cost savings associated with technology. Electronic communication cuts out the printing and mailing costs. Some associations are even hosting paperless conferences, setting up Internet stations, or providing wireless Internet access for downloading the speaker's notes.

Furthermore, it's often easier to get sponsors to foot the bill for technology expenses. Sponsors like to be associated with technology because it's cutting-edge and visible to larger audiences who are accessing Web sites and downloading information on-line.

Recruiting Math

Now that you know *what* your association needs to do to successfully recruit younger members, let's get back to the question posed at the beginning of the chapter: Is your organization afraid to spend money on recruiting?

Budget

Once you do the math, you will discover *why* recruiting younger members is so important and your association can overcome its fears.

Retention Rate
How many members do you retain each year?

- % Retention = # of Renewals divided by # Eligible to Renew x 100
- *If 920 of 1,000 members renew, your retention rate is 92 percent.*

Loss Formula
How many members dropped out this year?

- % Loss = # of Dropped Members divided by # Eligible to Renew x 100
- *If 80 members drop out from an eligible renewal base of 1,000, the loss rate is 8 percent.*

Turnover Period
This is the time in which your entire membership will disappear at your current loss rate if you obtain no new members.

- Turnover Period (years) = 100 divided by Loss Rate (expressed in a percentage)
- *With an 8 percent loss rate, it would take 12.5 years to wipe out your membership.*

Average Member Tenure

- Average Member Tenure (years) = Turnover Period (years) divided by 2

- *If your membership turns over in 12.5 years, some members are staying one year, while others are staying much longer. The average member is going to stay just over half of the turnover period.*

Cost of Serving Members

- Average Cost ($ per member) = Total Expenses ($) divided by # of Members.

- *If your association has $350,000 in expenses per year and a membership of 1,000 members, the cost to serve a member is $350 each.*

Lifetime Member Value

Knowing the lifetime value of a member allows your association to realistically determine how much to spend in a membership campaign to enroll a new member. The lifetime value of a member includes both annual dues and projected non-dues income. In the example we're using here, you have determined that the loss rate is 8 percent and the average member stays for 6.25 years.

Budget

Lifetime Dues Income

- Dues Income = Average Member Tenure x Annual Dues Amount
- *For example, $400 annual dues X 6.25 years results in $2,500 expected lifetime dues income from one new member.*

Lifetime Non-Dues Income

- Non-Dues = Non-Dues Income divided by # of Members x Average Member Tenure
- *For example, divide $125,000 in non-dues income by 1,000 members and you determine the non-dues income is $125 per member. Multiply this by 6.25 years (average member tenure), and you can generalize that the non-dues lifetime value of a member is $781.25.)*

Total Member Value

- Value = Lifetime Dues Income + Lifetime Non-dues Income
- *For every new member, you'll receive approximately this sum across the lifetime of the member's participation in the association. If you can keep the member longer than the average member tenure, you will improve the value of the member.*

Cost of Enrolling Members

Few associations know how much money to budget for getting new members each year. Once you know the lifetime value of a member, your association should be willing to focus additional energy and funds on membership development.

- Enrollment Cost = Lifetime Value - (Average Annual Cost to Serve a Member x Average Member Tenure)

In this example the lifetime value of a member is $3,281.25. Subtract that from the cost of serving a member across the 6.25-year period of membership ($350 X 6.25 = $2,187.50) to determine the profit for enrolling the member. In this case, if you enroll a new member who is likely to remain in your association for 6.25 years, the profit is $1,093.75. Compare that to the one-time cost of acquiring a new member (in mailings, promotions, first-year dues discounts, and so forth) to see whether your marketing operations are making sense—and making money.

Of course, there are many factors that influence the quality of an association's services and also affect the duration and profitability of membership. However, these formulas can help provide you with a new perspective when it comes to spending money on recruiting and retention—and pinpoint the estimated lifespan of your association without new members.

Recruiting young members isn't a quick fix, nor is it an inexpensive one, but in the long run young members will help an association grow. And that's an investment worth making.

Questions to Consider:

1. How much is your association willing to spend on recruiting younger members?

2. How many of your members will be retirement age (sixty-five) within the next ten years?

3. Is your association making plans to recruit enough Gen Xers and Gen Yers to replace the people who are retiring?

4. Do the member benefits your association provides justify their costs?

Here's an idea! *Lower dues*

The Toledo Professional Chapter of Association for Women in Communications (AWC) had been seeing a decline in membership over the past several years. While the association welcomed new members each year, current members dropped off the roster.

In order to beef up the membership of Gen Xers and Yers, AWC Toldeo lowered the monthly meeting price to $8 for first-time guests and offered a special one-year rate of $35 for new members to join the chapter.

The New Recruit

"Our rationale here was that many companies have limited funds for employee association membership. In our market it's an 'either/or' decision for employees to make between Ad Club, PRSA, and Press Club," stated Rebecca Booth.

With a lower event and membership prices, AWC Toledo was able to recruit and retain more young professionals because they had the opportunity to attend meetings, form relationships, and get to know AWC without investing a great sum of money up front.

ROLES & RESPONSIBILITIES

EIGHT

"I think when you're talking about recruiting or retention of the changing generations, any organization knows that change has to happen— and the older you are, and the more active your membership is, the more difficult it actually is to change the culture and the product."

—Lars Hajslund, International Jaycees

Who will lead?

This is often the most daunting question membership associations must face.

The staff is working at capacity and the volunteers are on the verge of burnout. Change becomes an un-obtainable commodity–everybody wants it, but no one wants to assume the risk or responsibility.

And that's when associations become stagnant. That's when associations lose focus and risk endangerment. That's when associations remain Boomer-centric.

The New Recruit association seizes the opportunity to move forward. This association knows that where there's a will there's a way, and it continuously takes the lead.

Appoint a Leader

Great associations start with great leaders, and the task of recruiting younger members is no exception.

Some associations choose to hire someone to oversee the development of young professional and student chapters and younger member recruiting efforts. Other associations expand the job description of a current staff member, while still others appoint members to volunteer as committee chairs.

Regardless of which direction your association decides, it is imperative you appoint a leader to take charge of developing recruiting efforts that are specific to younger members.

As elementary as that may sound, I have encountered associations that have Boomers overseeing the recruitment of younger members, which doesn't make any sense. I have also encountered numerous associations that do not have anyone in place for this position. Rather, recruitment is a staff or board-driven initiative, which results in getting nowhere fast.

The New Recruit

When I was in college, I had an internship at the National Association of College Broadcasters, publishers of *College Broadcaster* magazine. The association had a stringent policy that no one over the age of twenty-five could work for the association. And why not? When your target market is eighteen to twenty-three years-old, it doesn't make sense to hire someone who is thirty years old.

The same theory applies here. If you want to look like a duck and walk like a duck, then you'd better hire a duck to lead the way.

As soon as your association identifies a potential leader to oversee the membership recruitment of younger members, the New Recruit will inevitably ask: Why should I lead?

By reading this book, you've already learned that younger generations demand results. They don't want to waste their time on something that isn't productive or meaningful, and they want to know exactly what they stand to gain from a personal perspective, as well.

You can't successfully recruit a New Recruit without a purpose in mind. For the best results, write a compelling job description for the leadership position, keeping in mind the interests and expectations of this younger generation.

Start by identifying the need to recruit younger members to your association, and then explain how this person can help. The expectations of the position should allow the leader the freedom to build and grow the younger membership, such as:

- Planning professional development and social events that appeal to younger members;
- Utilizing blogs, podcasts, electronic communication, and other technology to reach the younger audience;
- Overseeing committee development, meetings, and associated responsibilities;
- Launching a recruiting campaign, including growth within the existing association's membership and outreach efforts to prospective members;
- Launching a marketing campaign, pursuing publicity opportunities via the association's publications and local media;
- Setting a budget in cooperation with association leaders;
- Finding sponsors to financially support the costs associated with hosting events and marketing the association to younger members.

Describe your expectations, as well as the benefits, associated with taking the position. Valuable benefits are professional development opportunities and leadership recognition, such as:

- Writing a regularly-featured article in the association newsletter featuring the leader's photo and byline;
- Hosting an on-line blog for younger members;
- Acting as the emcee at all events planned for younger members;
- Representing the association at industry and city events;
- Acting as a media spokesperson on behalf of the younger membership initiative;
- Obtaining a seat on the association's board of directors;
- Gaining valuable professional skills by taking the lead on all the expectations listed above.

If your association appoints a member for this role, extend a complimentary or reduced dues membership or give the member some employee perks, such as providing office space, access to the membership database, and use of a computer or laptop.

Support the Leader

No matter how dedicated your leader is, he or she can not single-handedly oversee the recruiting process. The most successful associations engage committees of young members and allow them to operate as their own entity.

The most difficult task of the Boomer-centric association is allowing leaders—especially young leaders—to have the freedom to make decisions without input from or consent of the board or staff. This association holds information and power close to the vest, struggles to recruit new volunteers, and burns out existing volunteers.

The New Recruit association encourages the participation of many and gives young leaders the freedom to lead. This association realizes that giving Gen Xers and Gen Yers the opportunity to organize their own initiatives under the association's umbrella is a win-win situation for everyone involved.

If your association strives to be a New Recruit association, start by working side-by-side with your new leader and not from a position of authority.

Recruit Together

Ask the new leader to consider the role of the committee and the skills he or she wants to employ. Work together on tailoring a job description for committee members and meet with and recruit the committee members together. This demonstrates the association's commitment to the young leader's success and still gives the leader the freedom to make decisions.

Provide Support

Equip the new leader with valuable tools and resources. From marketing collateral to office equipment, treat the new committee leader just as you would a new employee. Provide a binder with association information, such as contact information; annual schedule of meetings, events, and publication dates; branding and identity guide, including key messages and standard formats for logo usage, color palette, typefaces, etc. I also recommend developing two key forms, both available in electronic format for easy download and completion.

- **Committee Report**—A form to keep the board of directors informed about key committee work and help committee members tie all work to the annual goals and strategic plan of the association. Reports would be submitted to the board of directors prior to each board meeting. The form would feature the following fields: Meeting Date, Members Participating, Committee Mission and Goals for the Year, Key Tactics Established to Reach Goals, Issues Currently Being Addressed, Next Steps, Next Committee Meeting Date.

- **Committee Planning Guide**—A form to assist committees in planning projects and events. The form would feature the following fields: Project/Event Name, Primary Purpose for this Project/Event, Project/Event Description (including specific and measurable goals), Steps for

Completion (including planned dates for each step), Specific Committee Assignments (list of names and duties), Materials and Resources Needed, Proposed Budget, Income, Expense.

Make Introductions

As soon as the new committee is formed, introduce the committee members to the board of directors and association staff. Let them know that the association is there to provide help and resources and is enthused about their participation. Also, give the committee leader a seat on the board of directors. This demonstrates the association's support and gives the committee a sense of belonging.

Set Goals

Host a strategic planning session to help the new committee identify goals and a plan of action for the coming year. (Refer to chapter 9 for more information on how to structure a strategic planning session.) Again, the purpose of this exercise is to provide support and be available as a resource—not to direct, influence, oversee, or implement the recruiting efforts or committee governance.

Plan Recognition

Younger members want to be recognized for their hard work. Make sure your association has a plan in place for recognizing committee members well in advance. Examples of recognition include: organizing a party to celebrate a major achievement, distributing an ABCD (Above and Beyond the Call of Duty) Award, writing an article for the association newsletter with their photos, sending a card or flowers to committee members who are experiencing a personal joy or concern (birthday, surgery, birth of a child, death of a loved one) or work-related change (merger, new job), and, at the conclusion of their terms, award them with a plaque to display at work.

Recruit the Members

In the previous chapters, you have learned various tactics for reaching out to younger members, such as reducing dues, using technology, and rewarding participation. But tactics aren't what's going to recruit the younger members–people are.

Every leader in your association–be it volunteer, board member, or staff–plays a key role in membership recruitment. If they aren't playing a role, then your association isn't meeting its full potential.

Here's an outline, in chronological order, to determine who should be doing what and when to successfully recruit younger members:

- **Board–Set recruitment goals.** As a group, ask yourselves questions such as: How many members can we reasonably assimilate into our group? What common interests should our members have? Remember, quality of membership is just as important as quantity.

- **Membership—Develop a database of prospects.** The most important element in any direct marketing campaign is the list. It should be targeted (made up of viable prospective members who fall within your association's pre-determined age group— usually under forty or thirty-five) and clean (current contact information and titles). Your association's list of prospective membership should include:
  - Former members
  - Non-members who attended events
  - Referrals from current members (actively encourage them to make referrals)
  - Related associations' memberships
  - Purchased mailing lists
  - Related businesses (i.e., a banking association should have a list of local banks)

- **Marketing/Communications— Write content**. Send an invitation to attend an event or to join the association to the prospect list, highlighting the benefits of membership and including testimonials or case studies. The copy on membership invitations and applications, as well as all association materials, should always answer the question: What's in it for me? The copy should stress the benefits a member receives and how those benefits make it critical to join.

- **Board and Volunteers–Invite prospects**. Invite the prospects you know to attend an event with you. Follow up with an invitation to join the association.

- **Membership–Provide incentives**. Offer an incentive to join, such as a free pass to a local event or a reduced membership fee for a limited time. Also offer incentives to those members who recruit new members (association merchandise or reduced programming fees) or host a membership campaign tied to incentives such as waived dues for up to one year or gift certificates.

- **Board President–Call new members.** Call all new members within a month of joining the association. Provide them with an overview of the association's programs and services. Engage them immediately by requesting their help with volunteer activities. Invite them to an upcoming event and offer to meet them there. (If the board president is unavailable to make these calls, appoint a volunteer or group of volunteers to act as the association's ambassadors and make these calls.)

- **Board and Staff–Host a new member orientation.** Host a teleforum or post a brief tutorial on the Web site for new members to receive an introduction to the association.

- **Marketing/Communications–Provide recognition**. Publish the names of new members, soon after they join, in association publications. If applicable, also list the names of the members who recruited them.

- **Events–Provide recognition**. Recognize new members at events by giving them different colored nametags or nametags with ribbons attached to them. Introduce them from the platform and ask them to stand and be recognized.

- **Membership–Distribute surveys.** Survey new members to make sure their expectations are being met. Contact them with e-mails and handwritten notes at the three-, six-, and nine-month marks. Request their feedback.

Once a member is invested beyond the first year, they are on the path to become long-term members. Unfortunately, most associations make the mistake of sitting back and propping up their feet at this point. And as soon as younger members sense the slack, their interest in the association wanes.

It is an important thing not to take current members for granted—especially younger members. Here are a few suggestions to prevent that from happening:

- After they renew their dues, send them a personalized e-mail thanking them for their continued involvement;
- Conduct a special award ceremony at the annual convention or other program for five-year members (as well as ten- and twenty-five-year members);
- Actively recruit them to fulfill volunteer positions;
- Request their advice with new member, sponsorship, and speaker referrals;
- Invite them to contribute articles or give a presentation;
- Honor and recognize them at every opportunity;

- Continue to explain how their support and involvement can make a difference.

Does this sound like a lot of work? It is!

There's no way to get around it—your association's leadership is going to have to work harder to recruit and retain younger members.

Fortunately, the concept is simple: Younger members need to feel they belong and their contributions are valued. If your association can find a way to meet their basic needs, the younger members will be there to participate—and, more importantly, to lead.

Questions to Consider:

1. How will we respond to new members?

2. How will we respond to dropped members?

3. How will we recruit new members?

4. How will we re-activate inactive members?

5. What are our goals for recruiting and retaining younger members?

6. What three action steps can we take to meet those goals?

Here's an idea! *Never Give Up*

The American Medical Association's Young Physicians Section (YPS) was founded in 1986, when AMA first started to observe its downward membership trend.

Since then, YPS has been actively involving medical professionals under the age of forty in AMA's policy-making, communications, membership recruitment, and educational and professional development activities.

After years of tireless effort, YPS experienced its first real YPS membership boost in 2004.

How did the AMA start recruiting younger members? The organization started to rally around issues of relevance to younger physicians.

For example, AMA started to advocate on issues like patient safety, promoting healthy lifestyles, and eliminating health disparities, which are issues that interest young physicians.

YPS also identified ways to involve and recognize young physicians, such as giving YPS members the opportunity to lobby issues directly to AMA's House of Delegates and distributing leadership awards to young physicians, residents, students, and international medical graduates.

Furthermore, YPS created communications tools specific to its membership, including a quarterly YPS newsletter, weekly e-newsletter, and on-line roundtables.

PLANNING & IMPLEMENTATION

NINE

If you had to drive to an unknown destination without a map, you would probably get there sooner or later. But with a map, you'd get to your destination a lot faster.

That same philosophy applies to growth planning. If you want to be a growth association rather than one that is meandering through the countryside, you really need to use a map.

The Boomer-centric association shies away from growth planning, either because it indicates change and the association doesn't want to change, or because the leaders anticipate it to be a formalized, lengthy, expensive, time-consuming, complicated, and downright dreadful process.

The New Recruit association enthusiastically jumps into the growth planning process, eliminating all the formalities, bringing innovative solutions to the table, engaging its audience, and generating results.

The New Recruit association understands that a growth plan simply determines who the association is going to recruit, how many members it needs to recruit, and when and how it's going to recruit them.

The association that tries to engage its members in lengthy meetings and decision-making processes will squelch the enthusiasm of its younger members. On the other hand, while freedom is essential to successfully recruiting younger members, freedom without direction is chaos and members will eventually become frustrated and disinterested in the association.

Where's the happy medium? It's giving your members the tools to succeed and the opportunity to lead.

The Tools

Once your association appoints a new leader and committee, they must first learn about the association and determine a plan of action. In other words, they have to know their product before they can sell it.

Organize a joint meeting with the new chair and committee members and one to two representatives of the association—preferably the membership chair and marketing chair. The purpose of this initial meeting will be to immediately engage the new committee in strategic planning and answer any questions they may have about the association. The meeting should last two to three hours and cover the following areas.

Association 101

Start by providing the committee with a detailed overview of the association's mission and vision, services, programs, and benefits. You want to make sure they understand the scope of the association—where it is and where it is going—and how their participation is going to make a difference.

Communications Audit

Review all of the association's existing marketing and communications materials. This is called a Communications Audit. Do the messages and mediums appeal to younger members? What needs to be added, deleted, or changed?

Make a list of needed improvements, followed up by a list of tactics, the persons responsible, and a timeline for completion.

For example, your messaging for the New Recruits may be very different from your association's main messaging because now you're focusing on benefits that are specific to them. In that case, you will need to highlight the writing of new messaging for young professional membership and marketing materials on your list of objectives. That's an important objective, so the deadline for completing it would be one of the first on your time line.

Here's how it would look in chart format:

Objective	Tactic	Person Responsible	Due
Write new messaging for marketing materials.	Draft key messages. Review/edit messages.	Marketing Chair YP Committee	9/1/2007 9/5/2007

SWOT Analysis

In marketing, there is a tool that's used for strategic planning purposes. It's called the SWOT Analysis, which stands for Strengths, Weaknesses, Opportunities, and Threats. While your association may have done a SWOT Analysis in the past, this time around it will be different because you are now observing the association through the eyes of a New Recruit.

Start by listing all the association's strengths, focusing on those benefits that would be most relevant to younger members, such as professional development opportunities and technology.

Next, list the association's weaknesses—areas where the association may fall short of a New Recruit's expectations. Thoughtfully consider your association's competition, as well. What are those associations doing better when it comes to recruiting younger members?

Then list the association's opportunities. These are markets, products, and services currently untapped by the association which may provide opportunities for growth.

Finally, list the association's threats. This list should include anything that does or could endanger and prohibit the association's growth and success in recruiting younger members.

Once you've created your lists, you need to analyze them. The goal of the SWOT Analysis is to accentuate the positive and eliminate the negative.

For starters, go back to your lists of strengths and opportunities and determine ways to capitalize on them. Add to your list of objectives and tactics, and assign a time line and persons responsible for overseeing the completion of each tactic.

For example, your association may want to launch an e-newsletter. That's the objective. Tactics would include HTML design, content writing and editing, distribution, and maybe selling ads.

Likewise, refer back to your lists of weaknesses and threats. The purpose here is to determine tactics to counteract the weaknesses and threats and either eliminate them or reduce their impact.

For example, your association's recruiting efforts may be threatened by another association that has been successfully recruiting younger members for the past few years. In that case, your association would need to spend some time analyzing the reasons why the competition has been so successful. Then, establish offerings that are unique to your association, and actively promote what your association has to offer into its publicity.

Goal Setting

Also take time to consider the association's growth plan. Based on your findings in the previous chapter, how many members does your association need to sustain its growth and longevity? What are your membership goals for this year? Next year? Two years from now?

Upon completion of this meeting, the new committee will have a list of tactics and a time line for launching a membership recruiting campaign.

Phases Two and Three

Be advised that this initial growth planning process should not take longer than three months and should be limited to five objectives. Prepare only for the launch of a young professional initiative and complete the must-haves prior to the launch. Otherwise, your association is likely to burn out its new volunteers before they even get started.

Create a Phase Two plan for the three months following the launch, and a Phase Three plan for the following six months. Phase Two should be focused on launching the other must-haves that weren't completed in Phase One.

For example, if your association needs to introduce some new programming for young professionals, it should plan to roll those out or at least announce them in Phase Two. New programming, such as a career development workshop, is a priority because it is a tangible member benefit, offers a revenue-generating opportunity, and quickly engages the new target market.

Phase Two is also the time to focus on publicity. Start by contacting local or industry reporters to tell them about your new initiative or submit a news release to publications announcing the launch of your recruiting initiative.

Many associations make the mistake of considering media pitches and news releases as the only tactics for promotion. Not so! Here are additional tactics that garner publicity for your association:

Guest Articles

Write a position paper (opinion editorial) on an issue of related concern to readers, such as the need to recruit younger professionals to the workforce. Submit it to a publication your target market is likely to read. Make sure your organization and its Web site are listed somewhere in the article or boilerplate (biography) paragraph that accompanies the article.

Direct Mail

Send an invitation to your target market to attend an upcoming event or an invitation to join, highlighting the member benefits your association offers. A direct mail piece can be almost anything, from a gift to a postcard. Have fun with it.

Talk Shows

Hundreds of hours of free time on television and radio public affairs programs and cable systems can be used to educate the public, raise money, alter attitudes, and make a name for an association. The key to successfully pitching a talk show producer or guest coordinator is to mix timeliness with consumer interest.

Celebrities

Well-known people can spread the word in public service announcements, publications, and personal appearances. They are instantly recognizable, newsworthy, and frequently will donate time if they believe in the cause being promoted. Target local celebrities who are young professionals—television personalities, sports personalities, artists, business owners, etc. Request a personal appearance on your association's behalf or ask for the celebrity's participation in an advertising campaign.

Community Service Projects

Food donations, community improvement projects, and raising/donating money all attract publicity and helps to support your community. The donation can be small or large, but it must be genuine and heartfelt.

Media Sponsorships

Invite media to co-sponsor a seminar or awards program with your association. Your association gains from the complimentary advertising provided by the media, while the media sponsor gains exposure to your members, signage at the event, and perhaps a role as emcee at the event.

In Phase Three, focus on introducing new services and benefits that have not yet been introduced and otherwise strive to sustain your momentum. Also, take time to track your progress and celebrate your success.

Ideally, your new committee will want to maintain their leadership roles for the first two years after launching the new young professionals' initiative. This helps to reduce turnover and maintain consistency. If that's not the case, then recruiting and training new leaders should also take place in Phase Three.

The Opportunity

Once the growth plan is complete and the committee has a recruiting plan to implement, they must be given the opportunity to lead. This means allowing them to make their own decisions, manage their own budget, organize their own meetings and events, and work at their own pace.

This also means holding them accountable, just as you would the other leaders in your association. Give the committee leader a seat on the board of directors or at least request attendance at board meetings on a quarterly basis to report on the committee's activities and progress.

Give the committee positive recognition in the association newsletter and provide them with the opportunity to write articles. Appoint a liaison on the association board or staff who the committee leader submits updates to on a monthly basis and can contact with questions or concerns.

An association can do an excellent job of equipping New Recruits with the necessary tools, but if the association doesn't give them the opportunity to lead, the initiative will fail miserably.

New Recruits communicate, work, lead, and make decisions differently than any other generation. And that's something an association has to expect—and plan for.

Questions to Consider:

For each new objective, ask yourself:

1. Does this fulfill our mission?

2. Is this a member benefit?

3. Does the benefit justify cost?

4. Does the benefit meet the needs of our target market?

5. Is there an action plan in place?

Here's an idea! *Get creative*

The Oakland-Piedmont branch of the American Association of University Women (AAUW) developed a comprehensive, creative, and successful plan to attract younger women to their organization.

For starters, the organization formed a free networking group for young women as a separate entity from AAUW. Volunteers from the AAUW branch organized the group and hosted monthly networking events.

"At the events, the young women always asked the group for advice on networking, job hunting, mentoring, and career advancement. We would tell them about AAUW and other resources, and then invite them to an upcoming AAUW event," explained Laura Vestanen.

Members of AAUW created a Web site for the networking group, and also posted the networking events on the AAUW Web site, community bulletin boards, and local Internet bulletin boards. They also gathered e-mail addresses from inquiries and sent out semi-monthly event announcements via e-mail.

In addition to establishing the networking group, the Oakland-Piedmont chapter offered a group trip to younger members and the entire branch membership, realizing that younger women like to travel.

The branch offered an $860 trip to Paris in 2002, which included air and hotel fees, an AAUW member-ship, and a $50 donation. Six members of the network-ing group and fifteen sustaining AAUW members went on the trip.

In the end, Oakland-Piedmont AAUW recruited more than thirty new members within one year, most who were under age of thirty-three. Their recruiting ef-forts won a 21st Century Recognition Program Award from AAUW's national headquarters.

TEN

CONCLUSION

Just as there is a calm before a storm, there is an eerie calm among America's membership associations. Some realize the brunt of the storm is yet to come; they are scrambling to prepare and ward off the worst of it. Others are resting on their laurels–sitting ducks–that believe this shall pass, and they will survive it.

But this is a storm unlike any other. According to industry experts, associations who refuse to change their course of action will not survive this storm. These associations, they say, are likely to fold within the next ten—possibly five—years.

These are the Boomer-centric associations, heavily comprised of and reliant upon Boomer leadership.

In 2010, membership associations will lose an estimated 7.3 million Baby Boomers between the ages of sixty and seventy as they retire. As much as Boomer-centric associations try to ignore that fact, they can't deny it.

Conclusion

Your membership association has to change if it's going to weather this storm. You're going to have to stop doing business as usual and start focusing on the needs and interests of younger members.

Prepare yourself: Membership associations have not experienced anything like this before. Generations X and Y have completely different values, interests, needs, and wants from the generations before them. Their worldview, their priorities—everything about them is different as a result of their social experiences.

Generations X and Y will not respond to the recruiting efforts of the past. An entirely new approach is required for these generations. These are the New Recruits, and they want fewer meetings, less hassle, and more convenience among other things, but first and foremost they want exceptional value.

Today's workforce is working 130 extra hours per year, and one-eighth of the workforce is caring for an aging relative and a child under the age of eighteen.

Between work and family–who has time for membership organizations? Who has time to wait in lines at event registration tables, attend long or numerous meetings, or participate in anything with little to no return on their investment?

In their harried lives and pursuit for more balance, younger members are taking an inventory to determine what really brings them value and is a worthwhile pursuit. Those organizations that fail to deem themselves worthwhile will not make the cut.

That's what I mean by value. If you can offer younger members an advantage and an answer to their problems and do so in a way that your competition doesn't, with on-going, effective communication and exceptional customer service, your association will surely survive.

Your association's sole purpose is to bring your members success—not just the older members, all members. If you lack a program or service to meet their needs–add it. If you don't know or understand their interests and needs–ask them. If you're not sure what one thing your organization does better than any other organization–focus your energies to figure it out.

If you can bring value to younger members, they will never question whether a membership in your organization is a worthwhile investment, and they will refer your organization to their peers. In one fell swoop, you can increase your recruitment and retention efforts, credibility and respect, and develop your association's succession plan.

The mass exodus of Baby Boomers doesn't have to be a death sentence for an association. The opportunities for growth are endless. Just consider the other fact revealed in this book: There are YP organizations nationwide successfully recruiting hundreds—even thousands—of new members.

Success is possible. Difficult, perhaps. But possible.

There's a storm coming. Will your association be a sitting duck or a survivor? The decision to delay or to take action is yours.

About the Author

Sarah L. Sladek is a Generation Xer who has worked for and volunteered as a board member for numerous regional and national membership organizations. She started researching the absence of younger generations in membership associations in 2002, and has given presentations and published articles on the topic. Sarah is the founder and president of Limelight Associations, a strategic marketing communications company for membership associations, which is based in Minneapolis, Minnesota. She is the daughter of Traditionalists, sister of Baby Boomers, wife to a fellow Xer, and mother of two Gen Zs.